TAPESTRY OF MY MOTHER'S LIFE

Stories, Fragments, and Silences

MALVE VON HASSELL

Our life lasts seventy years, and at the very most eighty years, and if it has been delicious, it has been toil and labor; for it passes like the wind as if we were flying away.

Luther Bible
Psalm 90:10

CONTENTS

PROLOGUE
THE SILENCE OF ZICKELBART

"Do you think Zickelbart is in there?"

Distracted from my efforts to open the window, I glanced at my brother. He was poking around in one of the boxes we pulled out of our parents' closet.

"Zickelbart?" I laughed. "That's all we need."

Zickelbart was one of a host of ghosts we had inherited from our parents. You might say one can't inherit ghosts. But our ghosts were as substantial as anything else in the huge pile of things more politely referred to as the "estate."

The ancient air conditioner sputtered and groaned, reinforcing the sense of sitting below a laundry vent. Of course, my parents, inured to what they considered irrelevant minor discomforts, never replaced the unit. They got a new stove only because the old gas stove blew up; we later learned that the gas pipe had corroded. The refrigerator was a relic from the 1950s; my brothers and I finally pooled our funds and replaced it in 1987. For visitors, served tea from elegant silver tea sets in the stately living room filled with antique furniture, this insistence on frugality was bewildering and incomprehensible. For us, it was infuriating.

The window was stuck. It took all the strength I had to

push it up. The air from the city streets was warm and heavy with humidity. Yet, when I poked my head outside, staring at 57ᵗʰ Street and York Avenue, the sense of relief was immediate. For a few moments I soaked in the sounds of traffic heading toward the bridge, sirens wailing, cars honking, and buses hissing and squealing as they stopped and lurched forward again.

I turned back into the room. The acrid smell of my brother's cigars mingled with the fumes from a whiskey glass on the coffee table next to an ashtray filled with butts and crumpled up foil paper. Dust tickled my nose. Boxes were strewn all over the carpet. Pop music from a portable radio on my father's desk blocked out some of the traffic noise.

The contrast was jarring.

Until my mother's death in 2009, my father's library had always been a serene oasis. It had retained that quality even after his death ten years earlier. This room, more than any other in my parents' home, reflected a perfect blend of their respective sensibilities and interests, a marriage of two minds. Undaunted by tall ceilings and ugly air conditioning units, my mother had chosen simple grey curtains with narrow trims in reds and blues and painted the walls in a light blue-grey. She and my father spent hours hanging the etchings of all the generals in opposition to Napoleon, with a double-headed eagle clock in the center. Bookshelves lined the walls up to the ceiling and were filled with books ranging from ancient history to the French Revolution, Russian literature, the Medici, and entire shelves of books on German history, in particular the 1930s and 1940s. On one of the top shelves, my mother arranged a collection of Nymphenburg porcelain horses and riders, stark white against the blue-grey background, some with falcons on their fists, others with hounds running alongside.

My father's desk gave the feeling its owner had just left it a few minutes earlier, with its array of a leather folder, a silver inkpot, miscellaneous silver jars for pens and pencils, and piles of scrap paper he used for his notes. If I blinked, I could picture my father sitting over a book, so absorbed that he was oblivious to the world around him, while my mother placed the tea tray on the coffee table, covered with piles of art catalogues from her work as an art reporter. When she made tea just for the two of them, she used a pair of Meissen teacups, so fine and thin they were almost translucent, and the perfume of bergamot and Earl Grey or in winter a faint smoky tang of Lapsang Souchong filled the room. I loved the slices of toast and jam, an essential part of afternoon tea.

Now, my brother Agostino and I had to face the task of dealing with the liquidation of the estate. The time had come to clean the apartment and get it ready so we could put it on the market. I dreaded this process. In better days, while my brother Adrian was alive, he and I had often laughed and commiserated with each other about the task that awaited us, aware of the work involved as well as the emotionally wrenching process of tearing apart our parents' world.

I was sickened by the thought of pawing through my mother's things.

Tired and drained after having cleared out Adrian's apartment after his death less than two months earlier, I had reached the point where I wished I could wave a wand and be done with it all. I had already collected stacks of bills and records and begun to work through the mountains of paperwork piled up in my office. My parents' penchant for buying supplies that would last them into the next millennium, less politely expressed as hoarding, did not come as a surprise. Meanwhile, the contents of the walk-in closet, in family parlance the archive, far exceeded anything I could have imagined.

All afternoon, we worked on emptying out the large space. Trunks, rolled up rugs, cases of wine and whiskey, Yardley lavender soap, coffee bought in bulk, cans of tomato juice bulging with age, miscellaneous art posters, a wooden box filled with cakes of barrel soap, an unwieldy metal file cabinet stuffed with papers some of which dated back to the early 1800s, formal gowns, golden silk curtain panels, brittle and stiff with dirt, and elderberry juice containers ordered from Europe—we called it "ant syrup" when we were children. Everything smelled musty, coated with the dust of decades mixed with New York City soot that blew through the inadequately sealed windows.

My mother's presence in the apartment was palpable. Any moment she might come around the corner with the tea tray, reprimanding us for making a mess and eager to tell us stories about her day's adventures. It seemed inconceivable that she was gone. I loved her more than anyone in my life and by equal measure often sought to resist her powerful will, like a rock in a current, hard to steer around, and at the same time the source of endless joy and delight. We called her Mima, and just the name alone always evoked a sense of happiness. Many years later, I was thrilled to watch my son break into exuberant shouts of "Mima, Mima," whenever she arrived at our house.

Christa would have been the first to say that she had lived a very full life. And yet, there were tremendous losses throughout. When Christa arrived in Bonn, the young capital of the newly formed Federal Republic of Germany, in 1950, she had left behind an entire world. The land of her birth and her childhood home had become a part of Poland. She had lived through the first years after the war under Soviet occupation in what was to become the new German Democratic Republic, also called East Germany. Her father, brother, first husband, and many friends had died in the war. Many of her relatives and friends were displaced from formerly German regions such as East Prussia, Pomerania, and Silesia.

Christa's second husband, my father Wolf Ulrich von Hassell, had been gravely ill during the war, spending almost three years in a hospital. Many of his friends died in battle. His father died at the hands of the Nazis after the failed assassination attempt against Hitler known as the 20th of July plot. In the first decades after World War II, my father was treated by many Germans as the son of a traitor. Meanwhile, his sense of disconnect from postwar Germany was exacerbated by years spent abroad as a member of the diplomatic service.

My father's career as a diplomat took them from Germany to Italy, Belgium, and eventually the United States. After living abroad for the better part of their marriage, they made America their home, where Christa managed to embark on a second career in the latter part of her life.

"What are we going to do with all this?" My brother's face was smudged with dirt, sweat beaded on his forehead, and his hair looked in need of a trim.

"Did you know there was so much in here?"

Agostino shook his head helplessly. He had what I privately thought of as the "family mouth"—wide, with thin lips, with a vulnerability like that of a child, and yet with expressions that could range from skepticism and amused detachment to grim resolution.

His expression of raw bewilderment echoed my feelings.

"What are we going to do with all this?" my brother asked again, holding a stack of papers in his hands as if it were about to explode. In a curious way, he appeared to take delight in the sheer horror of it all, relishing every single item we dragged out into the open, admiring the untrammeled eccentricity. I understood the sentiment to a degree.

With a mix of chagrin and affection, my brothers and I had often laughed about my father's saving empty aspirin bottles for recycled nails (you never know when you might need them again), his careful harboring of spare decorative metal studs for the wooden rim of a Spanish *brasero*, the little piles of unused stamps detached from letters and dried on the windowsill, and his insistence that new shoes had to be kept in the closet for years—because they were still too new to be worn. He was shocked when my mother wanted to toss out an old suit of his.

"Look." Christa held up the suit for my father's reluctant inspection. "The fabric is so old that the lapels are shiny."

"But, Christa, it's a very good suit," he protested. "We bought it at a fine store in Rome." That suit was over thirty years old.

Now, Agostino and I contemplated the pile in front of us.

"I definitely want to take the barrel soap home with me," I said.

For an instant, my brother smiled, and we were united. Both of us remembered the big pot Christa used for boiling the linen dinner napkins until the water turned cloudy. She stirred the grey mess with a big wooden masher, soaked the napkins in barrel soap, and boiled them some more until they were pristinely white and free of all stains. In the summers, she laid sheets and napkins out on the lawn, rubbed barrel soap into the fabric, and watered them diligently over and over, until the sun had sucked out all the spots and stains. "I am turning the bushes into ghosts," she'd announce proudly when draping sheets and towels over the shrubbery.

"I suppose we have to go through everything." Tentatively I pulled out a bundle of papers held together with crumbling sticky rubber bands from one of the boxes. "It's letters." My father's handwriting was unmistakable. "Letters to Christa."

Agostino wasn't listening anymore. He was peering at the contents of a badly stained oversized German-style file folder. "Letters from the Red Cross," he said.

"What dates?"

"Nineteen forty-seven, nineteen forty-eight."

"Look at this," I exclaimed. We stared at bound notebooks and stacks of letters in an unfamiliar spiky script. "I wonder who wrote these."

My brother picked up one of the booklets. "This one has

flowers glued into the pages and postcards. Signed by...," he peered at the handwriting. "Heinrich? Who in the world is Heinrich?"

I shook my head. "I can't deal with this now. I have to go home." I closed up the box in front of me. "Toss the tomato cans before they explode."

"Do you think they were imported from Brussels?" Agostino asked with a smirk.

"Anything is possible." We lived in Brussels when we were children. Frugal and adverse to waste in any form, our parents never left anything behind on their various moves from Germany to Italy, Belgium, Germany again, and finally New York in the course of my father's career as a diplomat. "Why don't you start sending me some of these boxes? I will go through them at home. Will you be okay?"

"There is so much here—even stuff from before the war." Agostino was still rifling through the contents of one of the boxes. He looked up, grinning at me. "Really, do you think Zickelbart is in there?"

"I wish you hadn't suggested that." I shook my head, torn between laughter and tears.

On the way home, sitting on the bus in stop-and-go traffic on the Long Island Expressway, I thought about Zickelbart, one of our family ghosts.

Of course, Zickelbart did not properly belong in my childhood. He was a ghost from my mother's childhood in a place that belonged to the past in more ways than one. He figured prominently in Christa's stories about Muttrin, the place in Pomerania where she spent much of her early years. After World War II, Muttrin became a part of Poland and is now called Motarzyno. It is located about an hour west of Gdansk close to the Baltic Sea.

Zickelbart means "Ragged Beard." Who was Zickelbart? Where did he come from? My mother had no idea. This disembodied spirit appeared on occasion in Christa's childhood home, upsetting the balance of the house for days on end. The lack of details left me free to imagine him and to give him color and substance.

When I was a little girl, lying in bed at night and trying to keep nightmares at bay, I pictured Zickelbart sweeping through the house, his hands reaching out as if to plead and to repel, brushing the whitewashed walls with his fingertips. The pointy beard always appeared ragged and slightly tinged with green. The slippers were worn and floppy looking, too long as if running away from the bony feet, blue with cold, sticking out underneath grey-striped pajama legs that seemingly independently indicated the bowlegs of their inhabitant. I borrowed the silk pajamas from my father just as I imposed my father's skinny bowlegs on Zickelbart. His spread-out arms fluttered as he weaved through endless hallways, with staring eyes and mouth wide open, pleading without a sound, in the shadow kingdom of passed-on memories.

Zickelbart flitted in and out of Christa's stories often enough that it was as if I had known him all my life—baffling, inconsolable, and timeless, a melody haunting my dreams, as familiar as the warm earthen colors in the pattern of the Indian wall hanging in my mother's bedroom, stitched by a girl until the day of her marriage and destined never to be completed. Kept alive by her vibrant images, the country of Christa's childhood seemed suspended in space like the horses in Rilke's poem "The Carousel", hesitating for a long time before finally sinking away into the ground. And we had internalized it all; at times it was more real than our own lives.

Zickelbart remained a question mark as did so many other details in my mother's stories. Yet we clung to them, charmed by her enthusiasm and her gift for storytelling as much as by the world she conjured in front of our eyes. I loved the glow in my mother's eyes when she began to talk, altering her stories slightly at each retelling, never finishing anyone. The world conveyed by her words had acquired a life of its own in the memories of its survivors and our imagination—akin to a love that haunted us because it got stopped in its tracks and could never move forward, or the fragmented recollections of a childhood arrested at a critical age.

Sometimes my mother talked about writing it all down, but she never did. I am oddly glad that this is so. It leaves me free to play with her stories in my mind. It didn't bother me in the least that the stories she told us were fragmented. Their fascination lay in their being partially hidden as well as part of a world that was gone. A complete story would have been stifling.

The images of a magical childhood home filled with endless charm were all the more irresistible in that they provided a respite from the vaguely referenced themes of an insidious growing fear in the 1930s, war, loss of home and land, destruction, death of loved ones, disappearance, imprisonment, execution, starvation, fear, and exhaustion, on both my mother's and my father's sides of the family. It was akin to reading a book with disparate storylines on alternating pages, one with spectacular colorful illustrations and vivid details, the other filled with sparse commentary, references to experiences hard to put into words, and blank spaces. And yet, even as a child, while listening spellbound, there were times when I wanted to escape. The compelling force of these stories overwhelmed me and made everything in my own life appear insignificant. It was impossible to look away or fail to listen.

I should burn the contents of those boxes, I thought. I struggled with resentment against my mother. She had sat on all this for years. Who was Heinrich? She never told us about him. She left the letters for us to find. Wasn't it enough of a burden to know that almost every single object in my parents' house had a history and an emotional punch that could not be shaken off? I was torn between the overwhelming urge to shut the door in all of it, on the one hand, and the nagging desire to explore these worlds that were not my own and yet occupied so much of my thoughts, on the other.

The longer I thought about all this, the more I realized that I wanted to write down what I know about the arc of my mother's life—as a form of bearing witness and a way of offering the next generation a means of coming to terms with the weight of the past. I wanted to acknowledge the letters' existence and their tenor and mood, weaving them into the known facts of Christa's life during those years while adding my conjectures about her actions and choices. At the same time, I wanted to preserve the privacy of the writers of these letters. It proved to be a precarious balancing act between filling out Christa's remarkable story and respecting her silence.

When thinking about Christa's life from the 1930s through World War II, I found myself confronting contradictions and gaps wherever I looked. I had a few facts and a timeline of events, a few notes written by Christa while at university, a box full of letters, the majority of which were written by a man I never knew about, and her stories about her time in Prague, supplemented by a description of Christa in the memoirs of a friend. I was forced to piece together an image of her life from fragments she shared and the stories I have heard from others.

What struck me most of all was the fact that my mother, so compelling in telling stories of her life, became silent and non-communicative in important respects.

Christa's silence, in part typical for her generation, was also intrinsic to her personality. Throughout her life, Christa was unwilling to talk about anything that she could not manage in her own mind. She was the master of suppression and denial—in particular in matters where she fought bitterly against her inability to control a situation. My brother Adrian's nickname for her was "the queen of denial." Christa's survival instincts drove her to engage in something called *totschweigen*; literally, this means "keeping silent about something until it is dead," more properly translated as "suppressing something." Another expression that applies is *nicht wahrhaben wollen*. Again, the translation "denying something" is a poor shadow of the word, more precisely rendered as "not wanting something to be true."

As an aside, I might point out that the German verb *schweigen*, here inadequately translated as "keeping silent," connotes silence as an act of doing rather than a state. The notion of silence as an active choice runs like a drumbeat through the lives of people of my mother's generation, and it shaped her relationships with us as well as with others. We had a plethora of words and stories that disguised huge swathes of impenetrable silence.

Christa's life was not that different from that of many of her peers who came of age in the 1930s in Germany, lived through the war, and had to rebuild their existence in the subsequent decades. Christa was a product of her time and her upbringing, and her strategies to survive were mirrored by other women of her generation, in particular, those from a similar social class and cultural background.

The habit of silence on many issues, so deeply ingrained, is a common thread when looking at their life stories. I suspect that many were silent out of a reluctance to burden their children as much as out of an overwhelming sense of discomfort and unease in speaking about their roles as witnesses or even participants at a time when Nazi ideology permeated every level of existence, tightening its grip on every activity and imposing increasingly stringent controls over movement, writing, and actions. The silence lifted to some extent in the 1980s and subsequent decades, when more individuals began to write down what they remembered. These women lived through extraordinary times. Each of their stories deserves to be told.

Christa's story is also a universal one in that it touches upon the challenges resulting from relations between one generation and the next and the complexities of interactions between parents and children. We are shaped by those who have preceded us, especially our parents. As children of parents, all imperfect in innumerable ways whether present or absent, we are left with burdens to carry and to negotiate these in our own lives until we learn that we are also, if not exclusively, the product of our own choices. This too is a story that must be told to provide tools for the next generation to look back, understand, and ultimately move beyond the lives that have gone before.

The process of untangling the threads of my mother's life was inextricably linked to the impact her life had on my brothers and me. Of course, I could speak only about my reactions and feelings, even if occasionally the temptation to speculate about my brothers' was hard to resist.

Meanwhile, first and foremost, I wanted to weave as complete a picture as possible out of the fragments, real, perceived, or imagined, of Christa's life story and to capture the essence of this unique, complex, irreplaceable individual.

1

JOURNEY INTO MEMORY

CHRISTA SPENT THE FIRST HOURS OF HER LIFE IN A DRAWER.
I picture this drawer as slightly dusty and musty, lined with newspaper. It happened to be the top drawer of a dresser in a room in her grandfather's house, presumably with a faint scent of lavender and stuffed with her grandfather's fine linen handkerchiefs.

Christa was born in her maternal grandfather's house in Muttrin, Pomerania. Her parents were staying there in between the military postings of Christa's father.

On the day of Christa's birth on December 21, 1923, there had been a snowstorm. When her mother's labor pains set in, my grandfather dispatched Chauffeur Reimann to fetch the doctor. For reasons unknown, the chauffeur decided to drive to Stolp, the capital of the district, about sixteen miles away, instead of seeking the help of a doctor in a nearby village. On the way, he promptly got stuck in the snow. He trudged back to the house. After a hasty conference between my grandfather and my great-grandfather, August, the carriage driver, was instructed to harness the horses and drive to the nearest village doctor. Just like Chauffeur Reimann, August got stuck in the snow.

Meanwhile, the electricity had gone out as it often did when there was a thunderstorm or a snowstorm. Christa's father had to assist the midwife, holding a dim oil lamp, and after Christa finally made her appearance, her mother fainted. Perhaps her blood pressure had dropped after she lost too much blood. In the general panic, they wrapped Christa in newspaper and placed her in the drawer. When the panic subsided and they remembered the baby, they found her content and quiet in her drawer.

Looking back at my mother's life, it seemed a fitting and telling beginning. Christa had an uncanny ability to adjust. When circumstances required it, she was compliant. When she was free to act, she acted. When she could seize control, she seized it. When control was taken from her irrevocably, she created a space for herself within the confines life dictated.

"This dramatic entrance hasn't harmed me," Christa said with a laugh when she described the day of her birth.

Muttrin, an estate in Pomerania, had been in Christa's maternal family's possession from the 13th century until 1945. It included ten outlying branch farms. The principal industry was the growing of seed potatoes. There were thirty agricultural enterprises associated with Muttrin and the various branch farms, spread out over about 2,253 hectares or 5,567 acres. While there were a few small landowners in the region, a majority of the land belonged to the Zitzewitz family as well as two other families.

In 1939, the village of Muttrin had a population of 748, with eighty-five buildings for housing for workers. There was a bakery, a construction enterprise, a distillery, and an operation for the drying of potatoes, an inn, a wholesale enterprise for potatoes, a department store, a seed production enterprise, a saddlery, a tailor, a cobbler, a carpenter, and a livestock dealer. Muttrin was essentially self-sufficient; nearly everything needed was produced on the estate.

This included linen. To this day, I have dinner napkins and

other linens from Muttrin, where the flax for it was grown, spun, and woven. They were identified with red monograms and with numbers, i.e., No. 9 out of a set of thirty-six. The bedrooms were numbered to make it easier for the maids to sort the sheets and towels bearing the number of the respective room.

There was rarely a need to buy anything from outside the estate. Occasionally, Christa's grandfather went on a shopping trip to Stolp. Christa claimed that this happened just once a year. When he returned, the children were called to his study, and he handed out one single striped peppermint candy to each child.

Muttrin was typical of landed estates in Pomerania. However, unlike many other estates, it survived the Depression in good form. With tenacity and hard work, Christa's grandfather turned Muttrin into one of the most modern and profitable country estates in all of Pomerania. He initiated many innovations and improvements, including better bathing facilities throughout the village, a telephone network linking all the districts, and the construction of the railway line (Stolpetalbahn) from Stolp via Rathsdamnitz, Jamrin, and Muttrin, to Budow. It was built between 1894 and 1906, and it was in existence until 1945. As a result, Muttrin gained three loading stations in Muttrin, Nimzewe, and Jamrin. During my great-grandfather's tenure, new stables, barns, factory facilities, and apartments as well as a community house and youth center made their appearance. Muttrin was known for its social welfare network, good relations with neighboring farmers, and its reputation as an exemplary agricultural enterprise.

His son, Friedrich von Zitzewitz, the last owner of Muttrin, continued this work. He arranged for the development of more housing equipped with running water and an expanded electricity network. Water and electricity were provided free of charge to all working on the estate. He improved the roads and upgraded the telephone network so that he could run the entire operation efficiently from a central location.

Christa and her brother Hans-Melchior spent several years of her childhood in Muttrin and even attended the village school for a while. Until the last years of the war, she regularly returned to Muttrin for the holidays. From my mother's descriptions, I had the impression of seemingly unlimited space to accommodate all the aunts, uncles, and cousins, and other guests who descended upon Muttrin, especially during the summer months.

For years, my mother had painted an image for us, with her passionate words and her glowing eyes. In my memory, the center of that image shifts as if held in the shaky circle of a search light. The cone of light slides across the cobblestones of the large farmyard in front of the manor house, along the red brick wall enclosing the park, toward the façade of the house, where it briefly rests on the yellow wallpaper in the drawing-room. It hovers on the doors to the winter garden and briefly glances at the opening that led to my great-grand-mother's rooms so that one could imagine the short sharp bark of her snowy white Pomeranians.

The light turns, creeps through the park across the tops of the beeches, past the fruit tree orchard, shivers across the mound of the ice cellar, passes the red brick façades of the stables and the dairy, and returns to the entrance to the cellar where the large kitchen is located. The cone captures the trembling shadow of Zickelbart the ghost before he vanishes and the light flickers out.

Christa's descriptions were so vivid that it was as if I walked beside her when she came in from outside. One of her favorite haunts was the cloakroom, typical of manor houses in Pomerania, next to the entrance. It comprised an entire world of hunting, horses, and dogs, and smelled of leather, old loden coats, gun oil, smoke, and soap. Everything gave off an air of having been forgotten there and at the same time forbidden to the children—horrifying and wonderful in turn. I had no difficulty imagining Christa as a little girl, peeking into the cloakroom, and reveling in the rich scents.

The main house had two central poles, the office of Christa's grandfather and her grandmother's boudoir.

Christa liked to sit on a little leather stool in her grandfather's office, gazing at the rows of lithographs of famous horses by Franz Krüger above the desk and listening to her grandfather as he made his evening phone calls to the various farm managers. Christa's favorite moment was when her grandfather's stern voice relaxed. That meant he was talking to Hermann, the most trusted of the managers, on the branch farm Nimzewe.

The other pole was the domain belonging to Christa's grandmother. During the school year, when there were no other visitors in the house and after Christa and her brother had finished their homework, they would sit at the big table with their grandmother in her boudoir.

Christa's grandmother always worked. Her grandmother knitted or did needlework while instructing Christa in these arts. Christa knitted, while her brother Hans-Melchior worked on handicraft projects, cutting, gluing, and painting. The children munched on apples, and their grandmother told them stories—from her childhood, legends, tales, and best of all, creepy stories, some invented and some based on actual events.

Christa told us that during those times, her grandmother's personality came to the fore—she was relaxed, funny, and full of imagination. At other times, she understood her role as someone who took the backseat to her imposing husband. With infinite patience, she tolerated the entire army of aunts, descending upon Muttrin over the summer months, who enjoyed tearing her to shreds with criticism. Her calm response invariable was, "This is their home," while she tirelessly managed to take care of everyone in the house and beyond.

Meanwhile, there was another domain around which life revolved, and that was the kitchen, ruled by Mamsell Hübner.

Mamsell is derived from the French word *Mademoiselle* but was used also for married ladies as a form of respect. And Mamsell Hübner, the cook in Muttrin, was a formidable presence as the powerful and inviolable ruler of her realm. She was only thrown off balance by the periodic ghostly appearance of Zickelbart. On such occasions, Mamsell Hübner would be in a state of extreme distress for days at a time with dire effects on everything in her purview. Food got burned, milk turned sour, and the famous "Four Men Sausage"—why it bore this memorable name my mother never was able to figure out—was salted beyond recognition. When the children appeared in search of extra helpings of bread and cheese, they were sent away empty-handed. Kitchen maids trod softly, afraid of getting barked at, and my great-grandmother gave Mamsell Hübner a wide berth. Eventually, the crisis would pass, and the house returned to normal.

My favorite stories involved the food Christa described in mouthwatering details. I don't know what was more important to me as I listened—the food, tempting, mysterious, and appalling in turn, or my mother's evident delight. There was *Schmalz*, that peculiar German culinary specialty of rendered goose fat, allowed to congeal until it was a firm greyish mass. One ate it as a spread on bread or toast, preferably with a pinch of salt. There were goose tongues with apple sauce— apparently a Pomeranian delicacy. Christa raved about something bearing the evocative name of *Floom* which consisted of coarsely ground goose fat mixed with goose meat cut into small pieces and drenched in marjoram. She insisted that the oven in the kitchen produced the best bread in the whole world—warm and fragrant with the crust always just at the edge of being scorched. Christa and the other children in

Muttrin regularly visited the kitchen where they raided the larder for generous helpings of bread with cheese and *Schmalz*.

Christa and her brother were best friends with the daughter of the carriage driver August Schallock and the son of Butler Friedrich respectively, who shared a house within walking distance of the manor. August lived on one side and Friedrich on the other. When visiting Mother Schallock, the wife of August, Christa loved to peek into the seemingly bottomless iron pot on the stove filled with "pig potatoes"— mushy potatoes deemed just good enough for pigs—and covetously eyed the large green glass bottle on the counter, filled with gently fermenting current wine. The children were not allowed to drink it and as a result, loved it all the more. Mother Schallock always worried that "the children from the castle" didn't get enough to eat—a misconception the children didn't hesitate to exploit. In the goodness of her heart, she prepared pancakes; the children's principal contributions were a ravenous appetite, despite the just consumed afternoon tea and cake at home, and the eggs Christa had filched from her grandmother's chicken coop. The manager of the estate caught her several times, but never gave her away.

A child of Pomerania, especially a child who grew up on one of the largest seed potato enterprises in the region, Christa loved potatoes—boiled, baked with oil and salt, roasted in a fire, fried, and mashed. Potatoes freshly harvested in the late summer were her notion of a culinary paradise. Yet, to her everlasting fury, in Muttrin, the fresh potatoes went into storage. The old ones had to be eaten first.

For the midday meal, everyone in residence assembled around the long table, waiting for the master of the house. When his steps in the entrance could be heard, Butler Friedrich rushed into the dining room. Excited as if announcing the Second Coming, he shouted, "*Herr Rittmeister, Herr Rittmeister.*" Friedrich-Karl von Zitzewitz's military title, used by everyone as a courtesy, roughly translated as "cavalry captain." Upon taking his seat, Christa's grandfather began his customary inquisition. Had Emmy remembered to send a package of goose paté to Cousin Berta? Had she sent smoked pheasants to Erika? Had she sent a leg of venison to Vera? He went through a long list in this fashion, stern and relentless. Finally, his entire demeanor changed as he looked around for his grandson, Christa's brother Hans-Melchior, and said, "And how is my little boy? What did you do today?"

According to my mother, the "little boy" was a rascal with a penchant for getting in trouble. However, Christa loved her brother completely and unquestionably, and it never occurred to her to doubt the arrangement whereby she, the younger one by two years, was the one who would get all the blame whenever her brother had engaged in a misdeed. She told me later that she had always felt the need to protect Hans-Melchior as if she had had a premonition that his life would end too soon. He was killed in battle at age twenty-two.

Life was framed around the agricultural cycle and holiday traditions.

I could never get enough of her descriptions of the traditions observed during the Christmas season. Three large fir trees were set up in the salon and decorated with white candles. A few chaste ornaments enlivened this austere arrangement. They were added to console the children who preferred the gaudier decorations of trees favored by people living in the village. The salon was off-limits to the children until Christmas Eve.

Of even greater interest to me was an activity Christa called *finsteln*. This word appears in no dictionary; it has at its root the meaning of something dark and gloomy. Indeed, in her telling, it involved all members of the large household sitting around a large table in the dark while passing objects along underneath the table. Christa said that there was nothing as frightening as a glove filled with wet sand when you couldn't see it. My grandmother was particularly inventive when it came to devising gross and creepy things to hand along in the dark.

On the morning of Christmas Eve, the children took gifts to the people in the neighboring villages. Usually, there was enough snow on the roads for August the driver to take a sleigh, with bells attached to the horse's harness. Everyone was wrapped in thick fur blankets. The carriage rolled through the streets, stopping at all the branch farms, where the children delivered presents and ate cookies while August downed generous offerings of *Schnapps*. This in turn contributed to the increasing speed of the sleigh as it made its way back to Muttrin.

On New Year's Eve, an ancient ritual was enacted. It was supposed to ensure good health, prosperity, and fertility in the New Year. It involved the so-called *Neujahrsschimmel*, that is, "the grey horse of the New Year." Four young men of the village descended upon the manor house. They were disguised as a horse, a bear, a woman, and a stork, all bearing switches, which they applied liberally wherever they could. Their arrival was announced by shrieking kitchen maids who scampered up the stairs from the kitchen to evade pursuit. The four made the rounds of the village and received money and *Schnapps* for their efforts.

Christa loved to describe the practical jokes inflicted by the children on unsuspecting visitors. This activity had blossomed into a kind of team sport, practiced with great relish by participating adults, my grandmother among them. Some are familiar to me; for instance, I have on occasion helped my brothers sew together the bottom legs of a guest's pajamas and watched with fascination as they precariously balanced a glass of water on the doorframe, positioned to empty itself upon the entering guest at an opportune moment. Others were new to me, such as the idea of spreading sand on bedsheets or sticking a hunk of stinky cheese under the mattress. A favorite prank involved the application of fizzy powder to the chamber pot—in one instance, resulting in a panic attack of the guest in question who became frightened about his state of health when relieving himself in the morning and watching the contents erupt and turn bright green. Getting hold of a live rooster and hiding him in the closet appeared to border on the fantastical, but Christa swore that she and her partners in crime had done this.

With malicious enjoyment, Christa described the reaction of her Muttrin relatives upon reading a letter from an elderly aunt announcing her engagement and the arrival of her fiancé. Her exhortation to "be kind to Adolf," combined with the name which the perfectly amiable fiancé had incurred through no fault of his own, evoked unrestrained amusement among the recipients. Christa also loved to entertain us with the names of another aunt's children—Iris, Isis, and Osiris.

The children were taught the lessons of responsibility from early on. Christa loved the black pony, Pony Peter. The children would hitch the pony to a small cart and go on excursions all over the neighborhood. However, when they forgot to brush the pony, clean his hooves, or feed him, they found to their dismay on the next day that Pony Peter had disappeared. They would have to earn him back by doing extra chores.

One of the tasks delegated to the children by Mamsell Hübner, the cook, was to pick up fish from the mill at the branch farm Jamrin. The journey to Jamrin involved taking the pony cart along a long cobblestone road to the millponds. On the way back, the children often forgot to pay attention to the bags of fish. The bags, especially the ones filled with eels, had a way of slipping out from under the leather tarp of the cart. When this happened, the children had to turn back and round up the errant eels.

Meanwhile, sometimes when Christa was deemed to have been "good," she was allowed to accompany her grandfather during his inspection drives from branch farm to branch farm. During those excursions, she learned a lot about how to handle and work with people and to view the estate not so much as property but as something essentially on loan and to be taken care of and to be improved until it was time to pass it on.

All the children who spent time in Muttrin were taught the lines from Goethe's Faust, "What you have inherited from your fathers, you need to earn for yourself to truly own it." More importantly, they witnessed practical applications of this principle on a daily basis.

Christa's grandfather had taken over the estate in 1884 at the age of twenty-one, after the sudden death of both his father and his older brother. Initially, many of the workers on the estate questioned his authority. One story related by Christa illustrated his approach to such problems. Her grand-father heard a complaint about the lack of help in the cowshed. He nodded thoughtfully and promised that help would be there sooner than expected. To the dismay of the workers, he appeared in the cowshed at 3:30 the next morn-ing, cheerfully introducing himself as the new farmhand. Shamed into silence by the presence of *Herr Rittmeister*, or Captain von Zitzewitz, the workers turned to their tasks. They diligently mucked out the cowshed and pitched straw. There was a break; then the work continued. They milked, fed, and did all the other work that had to be done, with enough time for breaks. After three days, the foreman asked to speak to my great-grandfather privately. "*Herr Rittmeister*, I am glad to inform you, we can manage alone." Henceforth, everyone knew that requests for more help had to be justified.

On long summer evenings, days often ended with a walk to the family cemetery on the hill close to the Linden tree. Christa's finely honed sense for the ridiculous allowed her to enjoy a particular aspect of these excursions. The children would sing loudly as they walked, with plenty of Schmaltz injected into their voices, making them sound as corny as possible. The kitchen maids did the same whenever Christa's grandfather walked past them; they knew how much he liked it when they belted out *Waldeslu—u—ust*, with the vowels drawn out. The title of this favorite tune *Waldeslust* can be translated as "love of the forest," unquestionably a truly corny German folk song and to my amazement easily found on the Internet. Christa and her cousins played hide and seek in the cemetery and studied the names on the crosses, speculating about the personalities of the various individuals. After all, they knew their portraits, hanging in the salon where they looked down on all the festive doings from the vantage point of their golden frames.

Christa's grandfather was buried in that same cemetery in 1936. The Stolp daily paper wrote about the occasion, referring to "the old Muttriner's last journey" along the fir-lined path to his final resting place. Christa remembered the funeral of her grandmother, Emmy von Zitzewitz, né Blank, in 1941. Laden with wreaths, the coffin stood in front of the beautiful cemetery gate, while the villagers paid tribute.

Christa visited Muttrin repeatedly during the holidays until 1944 when travel became increasingly precarious. After that, she did not return to the place of her birth for fifty years. In 1994, Christa finally decided to journey to Poland, accompanied by my brother Adrian and me.

Adrian had bought a map that showed both the former German and the Polish names. Our Polish hostess, the lady in charge of the Bed and Breakfast in Stolp, where we spent two nights, pointed out the best way to drive to Muttrin. When she said the name Motarzyno, beaming at us in her kindly fashion, Christa repeated it after her, stumbling over the syllables and then trying again to get the pronunciation right. It was as if she was internalizing the name and accepting it for the first time.

It was like watching a blind person begin to get her bearings, at first confused and bewildered by utterly unfamiliar landscapes and then finding her way, with increasing feverish excitement pointing at this river, that forest, the little lake in the woods, the road to the mill pond, and the fields of her childhood.

"There it is," Christa whispered. "It hasn't really changed." Gazing around in doubt, her voice gradually grew stronger. "It's still there." Her frightened, tense expression gave way to joy.

Adrian and I had often talked about what it would be like to accompany our mother on this journey into the past. We were concerned for her and at the same time intrigued by the notion of seeing concrete remnants of her life conveyed to us so vividly throughout our years of growing up.

In the course of our journey, the distinction between what had been, what we had imagined, and what still existed became increasingly blurred. Our eyes absorbed the changes, eventually gently eliding them or dismissing them altogether while listening to Christa's voice as she described her childhood, recounting once again all the familiar stories.

Were my mother's memories of her childhood home constructed? Undoubtedly to a certain extent that had to be the case. And yet, these same memories had imprinted themselves onto our imaginations to the point where we experienced a sense of recognition in an almost visceral way—the sound of the trees in the wind, the way the light across the fields evoked the Baltic Sea nearby, the scent of the fishponds, the feel of the old red bricks of stables and barns, even the shadows of the alley trees, welcome in the scorching July heat. Christa did not need to show us the balcony from where the children used to gaze out at the park in the evening. We already knew it well from her stories. The fact that the trees were gone and the park a desolate wilderness was irrelevant. We recognized all this as if we had lived there—our own imagined madeleines consumed at an early age.

"You have to understand it didn't look like this," Christa kept saying anxiously during the first hours as we drove around the area. Like an embarrassed host, she apologized for the appearance of her former home—roads in bad condition, trees gone, buildings that had been neglected or altered or had vanished altogether, and fields planted with wheat rather than potatoes.

Inside the manor house, as we walked from room to room, at least in those areas that were open to us, Christa tried to point out where the furniture had been and what it had all looked like.

"This is No. 8," she said. "I was born here." We stood inside a room on the second floor of the manor house of her grandfather. The window looking out onto what had been the park stood open. As far as we could tell, many rooms were not in use, and this one was empty.

She apologized for the peeling wall paint and the misguided plastic wood panels affixed along the bottom of the walls in an attempt to fix up the house—apparently used as an administrative center for several years.

"It's fine, Mima," Adrian said reassuringly. "We have enough imagination."

I suspect in part Christa did this in a strange attempt to recapture what had been lost. When we were outside, the disjunction between her image of the past and the actual present was not as glaring, and she beamed with happiness at the wide expanse of the land, golden in the hot July sun.

We marveled at the detail with which she recalled everything. In the room that had been her grandmother's realm, the so-called boudoir, Christa quickly dismissed the unfortunate mint green wall paint, already peeling off in several spots. Instead, she talked about the Biedermeier furniture that had stood there and the green-and-white striped glass jar with a flower on its cover which had contained the raspberry-shaped bonbons the children were allowed to eat when spending time in that room.

With a tinge of regret, she mentioned that some of that

furniture had been sent to a storage facility in Stolp for safe-keeping during the war and that other pieces had been sent there by Christa's parents for the same reason. My mother used the term coined in Berlin for this sort of action, calling it *zerrettet*, a mashup of the word "to rescue" melded with "destroyed," essentially "rescued to death."

Adrian and I grinned at each other, relieved that we would not have to deal with these pieces of furniture in our lifetime and reassured because it was evident that our mother had regained her balance.

Wherever we went during our visit, living history surrounded us—in the form of concrete manifestation as much as in the form of empty spaces.

When we walked into the room that used to be the salon, Christa pointed out where the two massive bronze candelabras used to stand. By a stroke of good fortune, Christa's grandfather had given them to his daughter as a gift, and Erika, Christa's mother had managed to bring them to the West along with some pieces of property. Everything else that was still in Muttrin in 1945 was lost for good.

Christa never missed an opportunity to remind us that these candelabras together with other valuables had been buried in the ground during the Thirty Years War (1618 to 1648) lest we forget to appreciate their journey from Muttrin to Altenburg in Thuringia and finally to the West as proud symbols of all that had been lost. With six arms for candles, a Polish eagle head, and two lions standing on their hind legs, the candelabras were splendid and imposing. As a child, I could barely lift them. Sometimes, when nobody was watching, I would carefully examine them for traces of dirt.

There was the ice cellar—Christa claimed that it dated back to the Thirty Years War. Its entrance, while partially obscured by moss and vines, was still recognizable.

There were the ash tree in the park and the famous Muttrin linden tree on the hill near the old waterworks, both over six hundred years old. The linden tree, planted in 1555, appears in old shipping maps as a landmark. Our Polish guide told us that once a year, a commission from Stolp would come to inspect both trees, carefully measuring their diameters and noting this in the arbology record book of the town.

During our visit, the only time when Christa lost her composure was when we visited the old family cemetery. After searching through the woods on the side of a hill, we finally found it, nearly completely swallowed up by brush and weeds. A few remnants of a stone wall marked its location. The iron-cast gate and the fence were gone; the graves had been dug up and the crypt destroyed. Shaken and close to tears, Christa said that this wanton vandalization was pointless and of no use to anyone whatsoever; after all, in frugal Pomerania, it had never occurred to anyone to place valuables inside coffins.

Among many other stops, we visited the parish church in the village of Budow where Christa had been baptized and confirmed. The church dates back to the 14th century, even if the massive stone tower was constructed in 1646 to replace the previous wooden bell tower. A Protestant church since the Reformation, after 1945, it became a Catholic church. The neighboring families, all related to each other over the centuries, attended services there.

Christa showed us where her mother had always tied her horse when she came for her confirmation classes. In the middle of the churchyard, we were amazed to see a large iron cross, attached to a tree trunk. It was inscribed with the name Nikolaus Otto Dettlaf von Zitzewitz (1745-1804).

From our Polish guide, Jan Schloss, we learned that in the years after the war, when metal of any sort was a scarce commodity, this cross had landed on a metal scrap heap where it was about to be melted down. It was going to share this fate with a large bronze bell.

The workers in Muttrin had presented that bell to our great-grandfather in honor of his 50th anniversary as manager of the estate and placed it into a small tower in the park near the old ash tree. It bore the inscription "Lord, bless the work of our hands."

Our guide, together with several other Poles, decided that these relics should be rescued. They managed to retrieve them and installed the cross in the churchyard and the bell in the bell tower.

This remarkable effort to salvage local history moved us, especially because the people who live in Stolp and the region today have themselves experienced what it is like to lose one's home. They had been uprooted and forcibly relocated from regions further east, in particular, from the area around Bialystok, Poland. They talked to us about the challenges of trying to gain a foothold after 1945 in a region that had been largely denuded of tools, especially agricultural tools, and anything that included metal. The new residents had to begin from scratch as it were and also confronted life in an area where most of the vestiges of its former history had been erased.

Inside the church, the young priest welcomed us in a friendly fashion. He had been there only for four months and was amazed to hear that Christa had been baptized in his church. When Christa attended the church, it had been simple, even austere in its décor. Now it was much more splendid. The priest showed us the gallery where the old pews were still in place and pointed out the organ, half of which survived the chaos of war. It was fully restored. The pews had been polished and gleamed in the warm sunlight flooding through the stained glass windows.

Finally, he accompanied us to the top of the tower. The narrow staircase was badly lit, dusty, and hard to navigate. He flicked a switch, and there was my great-grandfather's bell, ready to call the villagers to Mass. Slowly we climbed back down; I looked at my mother from the side. Her cheeks were flushed, and she smiled.

Consolation comes to those ready to meet it.

The gift for laughter that enriched Christa's stories of life in Muttrin carried over into the present.

Christa was moved to tears with suppressed giggles in the living room of our Polish host. He served us Polish-style coffee, adding generous dollops of ground coffee into three glass mugs, and pouring boiling water on top of the grounds. This procedure afforded Christa ample time to study the décor. The large wedding photo, flanked by equally large photos of each daughter in their Sunday finest, floated above the sofa. Some sort of potted plant or rubber tree, lacy curtains, a large TV, table, and chairs completed the ensemble. Meanwhile, the crowning glory was the so-called Vertiko, a type of two-paneled cabinet popular around the turn of the century. This one had glass doors to better display knick-knacks. It contained the obligatory jumble of crystal ware, memorabilia, gold-edged coffee cups, empty chocolate boxes, and a jumble of souvenir spoons. Christa beamed at us, clearly struggling to contain her amusement.

Later, she explained that such cabinets used to grace the living rooms in villages all over Pomerania—a testament to the fact that the taste for knickknacks was not restricted to nationality. Moreover, the Vertiko reminded her vividly of the color print of a painting that used to hang above marital beds in homes in all the Zitzewitz branch farmsteads, Titian's *Noli me tangere* (Do not touch me) chosen from among all the biblical tales as suitable for such a setting.

For Christa, the fact that the house where she had spent part of her childhood was hardly recognizable did not affect her a great deal. It was merely a shell. Its spirit was rooted firmly in her memories.

In the 1970s, Christa found a home on the south shore in Long Island. It reminded her of the region where she grew up, with the proximity of the ocean, the sparse wide-open landscape, the sandy soil, and the golden light that appears in the afternoons. She was always on the lookout for roads where the street trees met in the middle, creating a leafy sun-dappled canopy. A potato field with rows in scraggly lines and weeds poking out amidst the plants earned her disdain. "My grandfather would have been appalled," she said with a sniff. She delighted in cornflowers, poppies, hollyhocks, and fields planted with golden barley. Wide-open swaths of rolling land made her sing. An old tree standing alone against the sunset at the top of a field filled her with exhilaration.

When I walk along a forest trail, I look at the smooth silver trunks of beeches through her eyes, and when I breathe in the scent of wet oak leaves in the fall, I can hear Christa's voice, reveling in the hints of red wine and wood smoke. Through her stories, I know the sounds made by the ducks on the village pond and the raucous honking of geese sitting on the fields after the harvest, and I can see the glory of the fine sand on the beach and the endless expanse of the Baltic Sea on calm days at sundown as if I had myself grown up in Pomerania.

On hazy summer evenings, when Christa sat on the porch of her house in Long Island, she liked to gaze at the dark juniper trees at the border of the meadow, their feet hidden in the fog. She often cited verses from a lullaby based on a poem by Matthias Claudius, "The Moon has risen," telling us how she and her many cousins used to sing this at night while standing on the balcony of her grandfather's house with the trees spread out before them like beacons in a silvery ocean.

The moon has risen
Golden stars, clear and bright
Fill the sky with radiant light.
The trees stand tall and silent
And from the meadow rises
White fog like a wondrous spirit.

The losses experienced by Christa's family were not unique. As many as fourteen million Germans left their homes or were deported from 1945 to 1946. Countless families from Pomerania, Silesia, and East Prussia lost their homes and their land in those years on top of a heartbreaking, bitter erosion of everything that they had believed about their country. At the end of World War II, East Prussia was partitioned between the Soviet Union, Lithuania, and Poland, Pomerania was split up between Poland and East Germany, while most of Silesia was transferred to Polish jurisdiction. In the course of the evacuation of German residents from those regions in the last months and weeks of the war, many lost their lives. Arriving as penniless refugees in the West, they had to begin anew. Nor are the descriptions of Muttrin unique—they reflect a way of life that was customary in those regions. And yet, not only are all unhappy families unhappy in their own way, to paraphrase Tolstoy; there also is a difference in the way in which each came to terms with these experiences in the years after World War II.

The stories our mother told us during our visit to Muttrin were characterized by several recurring themes—the march of time and the sense of an inescapable history jarring in its disconnects, a vivid recollection of foods, traditions, and the ingrained patterns of frugality that shaped daily life, a sense of humor and laughter preventing a descent into maudlin sentimentality, a clearly defined value system founded on responsibility for the land and its people, and deep abiding love of the land. In retrospect, her memories of Muttrin became the indestructible bulwark in Christa's emotional makeup—it sustained her throughout her entire life.

Upon her return to New York, Christa wrote down some of her thoughts about this excursion into the past.

"I hesitated for a long time whether I should undertake this journey or instead choose to leave my memories untouched.

Meanwhile, my memories have not been touched. Quite the contrary, they have been refreshed and enlivened. Since we returned home a month ago, I have thought of little else. I had not expected a lot, but I gained immensely. This may not be a prescription suitable for everyone. Each person reacts differently and has unique recollections from the sad to the beautiful. For myself, I can only say that I have not been as happy as I was when we were able to return to this marvelous landscape. Our grandfather has instilled in us respect for the land and work. This remains. This landscape has sustained our ancestors for generations. It will survive us."

2

DISTANCES AND EVASIONS

"I ATTENDED AT LEAST 12 DIFFERENT SCHOOLS," CHRISTA told us proudly.

I have not been able to trace this in detail. There was the village school in Muttrin. Christa also spent time at various schools in the towns where her father was stationed in the course of his military career. The peripatetic meandering from school to school contributed to an increasing emotional distance from both her parents.

Christa's mother, Erika von Studnitz, known to us as Nuna, was an elegant lady, comfortable as a hostess and with the self-assurance and confidence of someone who has grown up on a large estate. Her passion belonged to the world of horses, and she was a renowned rider who won many prizes in hunt races and other competitions, usually riding side-saddle. She was relaxed around dogs and horses. However, she was not a gentle person. She was uneasy with displays of personal affection and did not feel comfortable in extending such feelings. In her interactions with people, she tended toward the abrupt and brusque, leavened by a sense of humor. As a mother and a grandmother, she was impatient, and her temper was explosive, amplified by a deep voice.

Throughout her life Christa feared such explosions, exhibiting all the signs of someone who had been repeatedly traumatized. According to Christa, her brother Hans-Melchior generally was not the target of her mother's rages, and when he was, he found it easier to ignore them.

Meanwhile, Christa's father Bogislav appears to have been a source of comfort throughout her childhood, stern and demanding, but predictable, even though he was often away from home given his military career. He taught all the children in Muttrin swimming and took his responsibilities toward the children of his deceased brother very seriously. In letters to his nephews, he was thoughtful and considerate, trying to engage the nephews at their appropriate ages. Sadly, none of his letters to Christa survived the war.

Some of Christa's fondest memories of her childhood were of the trips she took with her father.

Bogislav took his daughter to see her first Wagner opera, *Das Rheingold*, in Zoppot, also known as the Bayreuth of the north. Years later, writing to a friend in America, Christa described this experience.

"The Rhine maidens, whose names Woglinde, Wellgunde, and Flosshilde alone were enough to rob me of my ability to keep a straight face, were manipulated on the stage with strings; this struck me as so ridiculous that it left me forever with a certain reservation regarding Wagner operas. Perhaps, I was simply too young and too stupid to appreciate it."

Christa also accompanied her father on extended travels to various eastern countries including the Carpathian Mountains in Ukraine, then part of the Soviet Union. Christa always treasured pieces of embroidered fabric that she had acquired during those trips, and many years later, when I went to Ukraine to adopt my son, she was delighted. Aside from the fact that she welcomed my decision wholeheartedly, it was part of a closing circle for her, further deepened by the fact that her brother died as a soldier on Ukrainian soil and was buried there.

Christa's formative years were defined by a simple life, governed by the rhythm of the agricultural year, with little emphasis on clothes or personal luxuries. Women who wore too much jewelry were derided as "bedecked with fat rocks," or as the "bling ladies." Waste was unacceptable, and children ate whatever was served at the dinner table. Christa and her cousins were expected to make do with whatever they had.

These lessons simplified life in the 1940s when food was scarce and when the known world fell apart and vanished. When Christa was already in her eighties, she shrugged off inconveniences or personal discomforts. I remember traveling with her and my young son, staying in questionable motels and eating on the road, always knowing that my mother would laugh and be of good cheer.

The critical anchors in Christa's childhood and years as a teenager were the times spent in Muttrin and the boarding school in Potsdam she attended from 1936 to 1939. Her recollections of the various other schools she attended faded in comparison.

As a child, Christa was largely oblivious to the insidious, ever-increasing reach of Nazi ideology. Boarding school also provided a screen through which experiences were filtered. Others of her generation, perhaps on the strength of hindsight, have spoken more openly and communicated more of their feelings and observations in writing. Christa never did so.

In a sense, I have come to appreciate this. Christa did not claim to have had any particular awareness or clear thoughts about contemporary events in her years as a young teen and was too honest to pretend otherwise. I picture her as a fun-loving, somewhat shy girl, caught between a volatile mother, a beloved but frequently absent father, and an adored older brother, and forced to change schools often so that her most important source of support came from her visits to Muttrin. Meanwhile, her experiences in boarding school, with its predictable rhythm and clear expectations, provided her with the framework within which she could begin to develop her personality.

In the early 1930s, girls growing up in Germany confronted increasingly stringent and invasive demands placed upon them by the Hitler regime. One of these involved the BDM or *Bund Deutscher Mädels*, the League of German Maidens. It was founded in 1930, and after the Nazis came to power in 1933, grew rapidly, incorporated into the Hitler Youth organization, while other youth organizations were suspended, forbidden, or integrated into the BDM. In 1936, membership became compulsory for eligible girls between ten and eighteen years of age. Members had to be ethnic Germans, German citizens, and free of hereditary diseases.

The BDM appealed and attracted young girls and women with the promise of time away from more restrictive home environments, romantic experiences around campfires, singing, and sports. It skillfully used these same as vehicles for indoctrination within the National Socialist belief system and to train girls for their roles in German society as wives, mothers, and homemakers, with an emphasis on the virtues of obedience, doing one's duty, discipline, willingness to make sacrifices, and control over one's body. The importance of self-sacrifice for Germany was heavily emphasized as was instruction in avoiding *Rassenschande* or racial defilement.

One of Christa's cousins, Ingeborg, known as Pudel, two years younger, was fascinated by the idea of joining the youth group and could hardly wait to turn ten. After the first time of attending a gathering, her mother asked her how she had enjoyed it, and Pudel said proudly, "It was great. We had roll call."

Her mother pressed for more details.

"Really? You don't know what that is?" Pudel gasped, amazed by her ignorance. "Well, we line up, our names are called, and we yell, 'Here.'"

"How long did that take?"

"About half an hour."

"How exciting. What did you do then?"

"We marched and we sang."

"What did you sing?"

"*Es zittern die morschen Knochen!*"

This is the first line of a marching song by Hans Baumann, "The brittle old bones are trembling." Along with the Horst-Wessel Lied, it was one of the most famous Nazi Party songs and the official song of the Hitler Youth.

The brittle bones of the world are trembling
When confronting the Red War.
But we smashed the terror,
For us it was a great victory.

Pudel's parents were appalled and irreverent in equal measure concerning displays of nationalistic fervor. When confronted by the vision of the little girl belting out, "The brittle bones are trembling," her mother burst out laughing, and Pudel's feelings were hurt. For a brief period, she attended events twice a week in the afternoons. Eventually, her enthusiasm wore off, and when her father was transferred to another post, Pudel quietly disappeared from the organization, while telling her new school that she was still waiting for her transfer papers.

Another cousin, three years older than Christa, described her disappointment at not being allowed to join the BDM. Because her grandmother was Jewish, Mareti was classified as a person of "mixed blood of the second degree," as set forth in the Nuremberg Laws of 1935 and hence ineligible. She also was not permitted to participate in sports competitions or the performance of rhythmic gymnastics exercises during the Olympic Games in 1936, organized by her instructor. She felt the pain of being excluded from her classmates and envied them their uniforms and ties. Meanwhile, her father protected her from further disappointments by forbidding her to sign up for dance lessons. Only later did she find out that she would not have been allowed to take these dance lessons anyway.

Maria, a close friend, like Christa was born in Pomerania, spent her early years on a family estate, and attended a boarding school for several years. In 1934, when she was twelve, she heard about the youth organization for ten- to fourteen-year-old girls and was fascinated by the prospect of sleeping in tents, hiking, and sitting around campfires. She was proud when she received the proper outfit, reluctantly purchased for her by her mother who thought the purchase to be an unnecessary expense but decided to let her daughter make her own experiences. Feverish with excitement, Maria rode her bicycle into the village and attended her first *Heimabend*—a social get-together. She remembered singing and reading aloud. The other girls, all daughters of local farmers, workers, and small shop keepers, mostly knew each other already and exchanged village gossip. Christa's friend felt out of place. Her use of High German and her name, which marked her as "the girl from the castle," presented unsurmountable barriers of class and culture. She never returned. In later years, when membership in the BDM became compulsory, she used various stratagems to get around that and managed to avoid being questioned.

In those years, the BDM acquired nicknames, based on the letters of the acronym. Some of these monikers were *Bund deutscher Milchkühe* (Association of German Milk Cows), *Bund deutscher Matratzen* (Association of German Mattresses), *Bubi Drück Mich*, translated as "Boy Squeeze Me," and also *Bedarf-*

sartikel deutscher Männer (Convenience Goods for German Men). Members of the HJ, in particular, liked to use these nicknames when talking about the BDM. The high rate of pregnancies among members of the BDM attests to the liberal atmosphere, in line with the stated goal of bearing healthy children for the Führer, as well as to the likelihood of wide-spread incidences of assault.

Sheltered as Christa was in some respects, I doubt that she was unaware of this. However, it is yet another aspect of her childhood that she did not discuss with me.

Christa never talked about the BDM. In retrospect, I realize that her silence on this subject was characteristic of her tendency to ignore or refrain from discussing subjects that she found uncomfortable, distasteful, or upsetting. She may have been a member of the *Jungmädelbund* for ten- to thirteen-year-olds, presumably attending events together with other class-mates from her boarding school. However, I don't know this for certain.

After December 1, 1936, membership in the BDM and the HJ (Hitler Youth) was made compulsory for eligible girls and boys between 10 and 18 in 1936.

In that year, Christa left the boarding school and joined her parents in Altenburg, Thuringia, where she eventually graduated from high school.

Several years after Christa's death, during conversations with her best friend Ursula, who attended the same school in Altenburg, I asked her about her own experiences. Ursula told me that she had avoided the BDM and somehow managed to slip through the cracks and that Christa also had not been a member.

Meanwhile, her descriptions of the boarding school in Potsdam she attended from age ten to fourteen offered some insight into her life in those years.

The Kaiserin Augusta Stift was located in a building

constructed for this school, with living quarters and dorm rooms for the girls, teachers, and other staff, a cafeteria, gym, hospital, chapel, and a special chamber set aside for patrons of the school.

A bust of Empress Augusta dominated the building's entrance hall. Empress Augusta, born in 1811 as Princess Augusta of Saxe-Weimar-Eisenach, Queen of Prussia and first German Empress as the consort of William I, German Emperor, founded the school in Potsdam in 1872. Originally, it was intended as "a home for the education of destitute daughters of German officers, military officials, priests, and doctors from the field of honor as a result of the war of 1870-71." In subsequent years, the school accepted girls from various strata of the society but predominantly from middle-class and upper-class families, especially daughters of land-owning families. Until 1945, an average of eighty girls attended the school every year. After 1945, the KGB used the school as its headquarters.

Dormitories, bathrooms, infirmary, classrooms, an art room, and an apartment for the school matron attest to an institution where the necessities were supplied while luxuries were disdained. Children were to be raised on the basis of principles defined by what was known as the Prussian tradition, with a premium placed on austerity, discipline, hard work, and frugality. According to a play written by Christa Winsloe and later turned into a film under the name of *Girls in Uniform* in 1931, some of the girls revolted against the unforgiving harshness of the school. Christa Winsloe also explored the interpersonal dynamics in the school concerning lesbian relationships.

Perhaps, by the time Christa attended the school in 1936, some of the rigidity and harshness had been relaxed, perhaps due to the publicity from the play and the film. Meanwhile, Christa throughout her life was comfortable and non-judgmental about sexuality for all that she was personally reticent in discussions. Christa at one point in passing mentioned the existence of "crushes" girls developed on others, however, did not expand on this, nor did she ever mention this play or the film that was produced as a result—and I failed to pursue it.

How and when I had internalized the notion of not asking questions escapes me. By the time my brothers and I were young adults, it was deeply ingrained—we instinctively steered away from areas where we might encounter emotional quagmires. We inferred but did not dig deeper. Only in the process of writing about Christa's life did I begin to realize the extent to which we had not asked questions.

Christa found the school to be a congenial environment and easily adapted to the parameters set by the school. The underpinnings were familiar to her from her childhood, and she had already learned the art of "slipping between the rain-drops" and retaining her freedom all the while. Following a set of clear rules did not present a challenge. As she explained to me later, it created a safe place. She formed a few friendships that were to last until her death. Unlike some of her school-mates, Christa received regular care packages from home and was happy to share these with other girls, not above occasion-ally using her ability to indulge in largesse as a way to create advantages for herself.

During class, she perfected the art of knitting underneath the table while not looking at her hands as a way to stave off boredom.

One source of enjoyment stemmed from Christa's perusal of the writings of an author popular at the time. Ernestine Courths-Mahler was a writer of romantic formula fiction, who published prolifically under various pseudonyms. Christa and her friend Helga amused themselves in writing in the style of Courths-Maler. Her unrestrained use of clichés both in terms of the language and descriptions as well as in the predictable template of love across social classes and socio-economic fortunes was too funny to resist.

Many years later, my mother cited choice phrases to me. She also devised new ones with the same swiftness with which she peeled potatoes, thereby forever scotching any innocent enjoyment I might have had in reading such books. I could never again read sentences such as "he grew as pale as the wall against which he was leaning," "her cheeks flushed with joy as her heart overflowed," and "his glance burned into her soul like the rays of the sun behind him," without bursting into laughter, half-embarrassed and half-chagrined because as a twelve-year-old I loved what was best categorized as super-market romances.

To my mother's credit, she made up for this disillusion-ment on my part by introducing me to a book entitled *Jubilee Trail*, a romantic novel by Gwen Bristow set in the mid-19th century. It relates the adventures of two women, one from the well-to-do upper echelons of New York City and the other an entertainer who worked in dance and music halls. Together, they travel across the United States to the then-Mexican terri-tory of California.

My mother blithely informed me that reading this book would help me with my acquisition of English. At that time, I had just entered eighth grade and completed two years of English in my school in Germany. "We'll read the first pages together, and then you'll want to go on by yourself," she promised. She was right. I was enthralled by the story, and it greatly expanded my vocabulary, some of which I tested out on my humorless English teacher. "Hell for breakfast," I proudly announced, also choosing to describe someone as "lukewarm milquetoast." Affronted by these expressions, the teacher claimed that they were not proper English, and I had the obnoxious temerity of a then eleven-year-old to show them to her in a dictionary. My mother laughed when I told her about this exchange.

Christa's stories of the time she spent in Warsaw left me with little more than glimpses of her life. She was twelve when her father was posted to Warsaw as a military attaché. She visited her parents in Warsaw on school breaks while attending the boarding school in Potsdam.

In 1936, Warsaw was an attractive, lively, cosmopolitan city. Christa remembered a stately home with a garden in a tree-lined neighborhood. Erika was busy with her representation duties as the wife of a military attaché. Her household staff included a cook as well as several servants.

I picture Christa as a slightly chubby girl, sturdy, but not athletic, with thick long braids, big blue eyes, a nose unusually large albeit balanced by broad cheekbones, and full lips with the tendency to look like she was sulking. I inherited this expression from her – one I fall into automatically when concentrating. Adrian used to tease me, saying it made me look like a frog.

In later years I came to see Christa as a person who was intensely private, but skillful at adapting herself to any given situation. I suspect that she had some of those same characteristics as a little girl and teenager, someone who learned to keep her head low when her mother erupted, while stubbornly pursuing the things she wanted to do.

So, in my mind's eye, I see Christa wandering around in that big house in Warsaw, sneaking into the kitchen to watch Lajos the cook prepare marvelous soufflés and elaborate desserts that emerged like minor miracles out of metal molds to be decorated and placed on silver platters bearing my grandfather's coat of arms. My mother must have taken internal notes on all this since she became a consummate professional when she was hosting formal dinners during the years of my father's diplomatic career.

Some of Lajos's metal molds and cake forms survived the war and made it to the West, and Christa used every one of them. To this day, I have a box filled with recipes that she got from Lajos.

A darker memory from Warsaw reflects the curious silence between the generations on some topics. My mother told me about this only as an aside.

Christa spent much time by herself when she wasn't watching her mother get dressed for a social function, marveling at Erika's elegance that she displayed throughout her life. She would run up and down the stairs on her visits to the kitchen, where Lajos worked on his masterpieces, and on one of her solitary journeys through the house, she was molested by one of the servants. She did not share this with her mother instead she simply took evasive actions in the future. Christa briefly mentioned this incident to me when I was a teenager, displaying a nonchalant attitude and also claiming that this happened to everybody and that it wasn't a big deal.

Did I believe her? I don't know. My understanding at the time was that the incident did not extend beyond a groping in a dark hallway. I also was then very young and immature, and my imagination did not extend much farther than that. I suspect that if she had told her parents about this, the servant would have been dismissed immediately, and Christa may have hesitated in taking such a step.

Christa's experiences in Warsaw became the building blocks of an internal handbook for her later life. She learned how to think of a wardrobe as part of professional responsibility, she learned how to run a kitchen and to prepare elaborate meals, and she learned how to avoid difficult situations while reinforcing her tendency to intense privacy.

Bogislav von Studnitz remained in Warsaw from October 1935 until November 1938. He was transferred to Altenburg in mid-November after *Kristallnacht*, the Night of Broken Glass, the pogrom against Jews carried out by SA paramilitary forces and civilians throughout Nazi Germany on November 9 and 10, 1938. Jews were evicted from their homes, forced to surrender the title to these homes, and eventually taken to concentration camps. Some Jews managed to emigrate, but many others were killed in the camps.

In the winter of 1938, Christa's parents moved into an apartment in a stately mansion at Bismarckstrasse 2. There were four apartments altogether, all assigned to officers in the army. One of these was the father of Christa's closest friend Ursula.

Christa left the boarding school in Potsdam and arrived in Altenburg in 1939 at age fourteen. She had already emerged from the chrysalis of a little girl and had matured into a self-assured young lady. In conversations after Christa's death, Ursula described meeting Christa for the first time when she was walking along the street with her parents in the neighborhood where they both lived. Ursula was intimidated, certain that this elegant and poised young lady would not have any time for her. However, they soon became friends.

When I researched the address Bismarckstrasse 2, I discovered that the house had belonged to a renowned Jewish family Cohn, owners of the famous Altenburg department store M. & S. Cohn. During the night of Kristallnacht, Albert Levy was forced into a truck and taken to Buchenwald. The house was ransacked, and the other family members were brutally beaten. He was released after agreeing to cede title to his house to the NSDAP. The family had already been forced to sell the department store in July 1938. Albert Levy and his wife and several children managed to reach Holland in the hopes of eventually traveling to the US. However, in 1943, they were discovered and deported to Auschwitz.

The surviving children of Albert Levy donated the house at Bismarckstrasse 2, today called Rudolf-Breitscheid-Strasse, to the city of Altenburg for charitable purposes.

"I don't remember thinking about this," Ursula told me. "I

don't think we were even told the names of the previous owners." She added, "I used to walk to school with some girls from the neighborhood—this was before Christa came. One day they were gone; I thought they had changed schools."

When Kristallnacht happened, Christa was in Potsdam. Perhaps she was not directly exposed or a witness to such scenes, given her secluded life within the confines of the boarding school.

Only in retrospect, as I began to piece together more details of her life during those years, I puzzled over my failure to ask while she was alive.

Meanwhile, another incident reflected Christa's growing awareness of the political reality. The so-called Blomberg-Fritsch crisis around two essentially manufactured scandals in early 1938 ultimately led to Hitler's ability to exert greater control over the German Armed Forces. Hitler had regarded both Blomberg and Fritsch, both high-ranking officers, as too hesitant towards the war preparations that he was demanding. When he learned about salacious stories regarding Blomberg's wife, he eagerly exploited this as conduct unbecoming a man in Blomberg's position and forced Blomberg to resign. Inspired by the results of this scandal, Hermann Göring and Heinrich Himmler decided to arrange a similar scandal for then Commander in Chief Werner von Fritsch.

Upon Fritsch's resignation, Hitler began the process of reorganizing the command structure of the armed forces and took further advantage of the situation by replacing several generals and ministers with men more loyal to him. The charges against Fritsch were later proved to have been false, but Fritsch, despite the support of senior officers of the Wehrmacht, never recovered from the allegations against him. Although the army demanded his rehabilitation and restoration to his former command, Hitler agreed only to name him honorary colonel of an artillery regiment. Despite the treatment that he had experienced, Fritsch remained loyal to the

Nazi regime and embraced some of its goals, most notably regarding anti-Semitism. Meanwhile, shortly after the German invasion of Poland, during an inspection of front-line troops, Fritsch was shot in the leg by a Polish sharpshooter and bled to death.

Christa described her father's disgust at the use of personal character assassination to destroy a fellow officer's career even though he didn't share Fritsch's beliefs.

Ironically, my Hassell grandfather had attempted to recruit Fritsch for the resistance against Hitler but failed. Fritsch told him that he believed Hitler was Germany's destiny and that nothing could be done to change the fact.

Christa offered a vivid image of my grandfather's reaction to Hitler's announcement of the invasion of Poland in September 1939. "This is the beginning of the end," he told Christa, pale with shock.

Christa graduated from high school in Altenburg in early 1942. Her matriculation certificate, dated February 25, 1942, included a short assessment, describing Christa as "measured [in her bearing] and even-tempered. She made a valiant effort when it came to physical exercise. She participated enthusiastically during classes. Her preference and strong points lean toward the world of art and writing."

I was amused by her grades since they mirrored my own. Christa had earned an 'adequate' in math and chemistry as well as in sports. I shared that reluctance with her as well as an appreciation for the written word. The world of art, meanwhile, is one where I have as yet to find a key. For Christa, on the other hand, it became a passion, strong enough to sustain her during challenging times and furthering her ability to compartmentalize and block off all the areas in her life that she could not control.

Her father and her brother both served at the front; she feared for them every day. Even more, she feared her mother's moods and her temper. Just eighteen years old, Christa was determined to become independent. She wasted no time after receiving her matriculation certificate and applied for a *Studienplatz* (study place) at university. She received permission to attend the University of Leipzig and matriculated in April 1942, while her mother remained in Altenburg.

3

RATION CARDS, CENSORSHIP,
AND COMPULSORY LABOR

FROM 1939 ON, LIFE WAS GOVERNED BY RATION CARDS, A
relentless stream of propaganda, increasingly stringent censorship, and the obligatory labor service.

Alert to the lessons from World War I, the Nazi regime had started to prepare several years before the start of the war by building a stockpile of reserves and introducing ration cards.

By September 1939, one needed a ration card for the purchase of milk, cheese, sugar, butter, fat, meat, and jam. Bread and eggs were added later. For civilians, a ration card for textiles was introduced in October 1939. Increasingly, food consisted of potatoes, grains, and flour, while meat had become a luxury. *Ersatzkaffee*, i.e., substitute coffee, was made of barley and acorns. People baked cake with potatoes or carrots and made jam from rutabagas.

However, there were no serious nutritional deficits in Germany during the war—to the detriment of the occupied countries. These were ruthlessly exploited to the point that there was little left for the inhabitants, and it resulted in deaths by starvation in many areas of Eastern Europe.

Military mail was remarkably efficient until the last year of the war, and soldiers in the field welcomed letters and packages from home, appreciative of warm socks, underwear, and news from their families. While mail was sacrosanct and its delivery well organized, as the war continued, guards had to protect mail transports to reduce incidences of theft. Theft became more prevalent during times of scarcity. However, Christa never talked about any problems with the packages she sent to the field, and she sent many, often in response to requests such as, "Please send socks," or "Could you find warm underwear?"

The most remarkable of these field packages was the *Muttriner Torte*, a special cake based on a family recipe. Ration cards and increasing scarcity notwithstanding, Christa repeatedly sent such a cake to her father.

Christa spent many months gathering enough flour, butter, rum, and jam before proceeding with the production. The cake consists of at least fourteen layers of thin pastry, individually baked, with different jams spread on each layer. Once all the layers have been baked and stacked on top of each other, the entire construct is placed on a platter to rest for several weeks. Subsequently, it is trimmed until it forms a perfect platter-sized round cake, about four to five inches in height. Gorgeous like a striated canyon wall in colors ranging from dark purple to golden orange, unbelievably rich, and presented in thin slices, it is a delicacy. Given the presence of generous dollops of rum in the dough, the cake kept indefinitely and hence easily survived its long journey to the field.

Christa showed me how to make this concoction. It is a project that takes an entire day. When I grew up, the Muttriner Torte appeared on "big birthdays" and other special occasions. We even made it for my grandmother's 80th birthday, transporting it to Bonn from New York City in a duffle bag.

I loved the Muttriner Torte for its taste as much as for the descriptions it evoked from my mother, and I liked to envision the cake, wrapped in towels, and placed in a box, traveling from one field outpost to the next in search of my grandfather.

Another central element of daily life was the increasingly stringent censorship.

Since 1934, there already existed the so-called Treachery Act (*Heimtückegesetz*) of 1934. Its official title was the "Law against Treacherous Attacks on the State and Party and for the Protection of Party Uniforms." It established penalties for the abuse of Nazi Party badges and uniforms, restricted the right to freedom of speech, and criminalized all remarks deemed to cause damage to the welfare of the Third Reich, the prestige of the Nazi government, or the Nazi Party.

During World War II, several facets affected letter writing. One concerned the regime's effort to control any form of writing deemed treacherous or seditious. Furthermore, propaganda efforts included the notion of letters as "weapons" that would help to transmit the ideology of National Socialism. Thus, letters from home were not supposed to contain references to problems of any sort. Letters written by soldiers could not contain any references to location, casualties, or other aspects of military campaigns; moreover, they had to convey a positive attitude and include exhortations to hold out.

Censorship during war times was nothing new, and most countries practiced one form or another. During World War II, both the Allies and Axis instituted postal censorship of civil mail. In the US, from December 1941 until August 1945, every letter that traveled into or out of the country could be opened and reviewed. The most stringent measures were directed toward soldiers' letters. Soldiers, in their attempts to evade control, would ask friends to post their letters once they got home. In Germany, such voluntary "postmen" were severely punished when caught.

Any writer of a letter deemed as *Wehrkraftzersetzung*, that is, seditious or subversive activities affecting the armed forces, could be punished by imprisonment or death. The number of such judgements meted out to authors of letters from the field is estimated at 30,000 to 40,000.

In addition to having to contend with censorship by the regime, soldiers subjected themselves to their own form of censorship in withholding details about their lives and the gruesome reality of events at the front since they did not want to upset their family and friends even more.

Letter writing to soldiers at the front carried similar burdens. Writers tried not to worry soldiers with too many details about bomb attacks, destruction, or food shortages.

Often writers pleaded with recipients to share details of a letter with family members and others in the fear that letters might get lost or would not find them because their homes had been bombed out. Christa, with her address in Altenburg as yet unchanged, often assumed the role of a general post office box, relaying messages and in turn communicating about the well-being of friends and relatives to soldiers in the field.

Meanwhile, personal communications represented another minefield.

Every letter written by a soldier could be a *memento mori*. How do you respond to someone on the front who talks about the future, the family he hopes to have, the children he plans to raise, the love he has for you, and the trust and faith he has in you despite not having received any mail for a while? Your words might be the last that soldier ever gets to read. How do you dare to talk about doubts or fears? How do you tell someone you have changed your mind? How do you say that you have met someone else?

In one of her few comments about this time of her life, Christa pointed out how hard it was to reject offers of marriage from people about to return to the front. She never mentioned any specifics, and I didn't ask.

Many years later, Christa and I watched the BBC television series based on Vera Brittain's *Testament of Youth*. It is a first-hand account of a woman coming of age in World War I. She falls in love and gets engaged to a man who is killed in action. Subsequently, she offers to marry a friend who was gravely wounded and blinded for life. Like Christa, she was at university. When her friends joined up, she decided to serve as a Red Cross nurse. All of her friends and also her brother were killed in action. For Vera Brittain and Christa, letter writing was a lifeline, not only as a means of communication and a source of solace and comfort, but also as a temporary retreat into a known world of literature, poetry, and art, and a bulwark behind which to hide thoughts and emotions from the censor as much as from the recipients and from oneself. My mother was moved by the book and the film version. However, I did not fully appreciate the extent to which there were parallels until I began to work my way through Christa's papers after her death.

Christa came of age in a time when censorship was an ingrained part of everyday life—as expected, unavoidable, and unsurprising as the *Die Deutsche Wochenschau* ("The German Weekly Review") before any movie, shown in cinemas from 1940 to the end of World War II, an instrument for the mass distribution of Nazi propaganda at war, disguised as a newsreel.

At the beginning of the war, newsreels would still report about victories, but as time passed, mention of such events decreased even though the tenor of newsreels remained for the most part positive.

My father described to me how he would go to the movies to watch this newsreel since generally news was hard to come by. He learned to read between the lines and to "translate" what was presented. As long as one assumed that it was all a lie, one could learn quite a lot. "Our soldiers fought a major battle on the Eastern Front and displayed extraordinary valor," could be translated as major losses and large numbers of casualties. "The front line is advancing steadily," could be read as a retreat. "Soldiers valiantly holding the line," meant the beginnings of a devastating rout. My father combined what he gleaned out of carefully coded letters from his friends in the military with what he saw during the weekly propaganda newsreels as well as from conversations with his father, a member of the resistance group against Hitler. After the Battle of Stalingrad in 1943, the increased efforts to control and manipulate the news were countered by eyewitness reports of soldiers as well as by *Feindsender* radio stations (enemy radio stations) such as the BBC, Radio Moscow, Voice of America, and Vatican Radio, even though listening to such stations was punishable with imprisonment.

One lived with censorship and propaganda and adjusted to it just as one became used to the mind-numbing sound of air raid warnings. The propaganda network, combined with stringent controls over any expression of opinions, in particular, through censorship, was so extensive and so complete that many people continued to believe in the final victory even until the very end. Meanwhile, when reading letters from the field with references to the hope that the final victory was near among other such spoutings of Nazi propaganda, it is difficult to distinguish between the embrace of Nazi ideology and propaganda and the fear of reprisal for oneself or the recipient if a letter was opened.

Another aspect of life was the *Reichsarbeitsdienst* (National Labor Service), which had become compulsory at the beginning of World War II. The *Reichsarbeitsdienst* or RAD was a major organization established in Nazi Germany in 1935 as an agency to help mitigate the effects of unemployment on the German economy, militarize the workforce, and indoctrinate it with Nazi ideology. As the official state labor service, it was divided into separate sections for men and women. According to the law, all young Germans, both men and women, had to serve for six months. However, as the war went on, this compulsory service was extended, and by 1941, the required period of service was one year, and in April 1944, eighteen months.

For women, the RAD was the logical extension of the BDM, which increasingly transformed into an organization to aid the war effort. The BDM engaged in the organization of rest homes and arrangements for sending children away from urban centers which were more liable to bomb attacks. It supported actions to write letters to soldiers or send them care packages. Starting in 1938, all unmarried women under the age of twenty-five were supposed to serve for one year in homework, care for soldiers, harvest work, air-raid protection, or communications. Like the BDM, the RAD represented a central component of education under National Socialism. Many young women became *Blitzmädel* (*Wehrmachthelferin* or female combat soldiers) during World War II.

In order to be allowed to matriculate at university, prospective students had to comply with the requirements of the RAD. Any laws and regulations protecting workers as well as any rights to benefits in the event of an illness were considered as not applicable to workers under the RAD umbrella. Hence, young people could be employed at low wages and subjected to intimidation at all levels.

The idea of national service by women was not originated by the Nazis. It had been introduced by Therese Cabarrus-Fontenay as early as 1794. It is ironic that the Nazis, who detested most aspects of the French Revolution, embraced this notion of service and turned it into a cornerstone of indoctrination and institutionalized exploitation. In Germany, it started as a form of voluntary commitment during World War I, for instance under the auspices of the Red Cross.

Many young women, including Christa's friend Maria, initially considered RAD an attractive opportunity for experiencing new areas of work, learning about unfamiliar aspects of the country and its industries, and exposure to different social strata.

Among Christa's papers, I found several certificates attesting to her RAD work, in stints of a few weeks, from 1942 until 1945. As far as I can piece it together, she completed these compulsory periods during her semester breaks. In December 1942, she received a certificate from the organization *Kriegseinsatz der Deutschen Studentenschaft* (War-Time Employment of German Students) of the University of Tübingen, thanking Christa for her service in "working toward the final victory."

Two certificates from the late summer of 1942 attest to Christa's work at Hugo Schneider Aktiengesellschaft, Altenburg. In her first stint of several weeks, she was employed as a machine worker; her certificate for her second stint states that she worked in a monitoring or supervisory role. Christa once told me in an aside that she was forced to make cartridge cases in a factory during the war. I did not realize that this was HASAG until I started researching for this book.

HASAG, also known as Hugo Schneider AG, was a German metal goods manufacturer founded in 1863. Based in Leipzig, it grew from a small business making lamps and other small metal products by hand into a large factory and publicly traded company that sold its wares in several countries. During the Second World War, HASAG became a Nazi arms-manufacturing conglomerate with dozens of factories across German-occupied Europe. Initially, HASAG employed civilian workers, men and women from all over Europe, especially from Slavic countries. Some chose to work for HASAG, but the majority were forced laborers; by 1941, HASAG was employing a large number of Polish and Croatian workers, and in subsequent years it also employed French and Russian workers. Starting in 1944, HASAG began to use slave labor on a massive scale. Tens of thousands of Jews from Poland, and other prisoners, died producing munition for HASAG in various forced labor camps in different towns around Leipzig with good rail and road connections to the main factory in

Leipzig. One of these subcamps was located on the outskirts of Altenburg. They died as a result of extreme malnutrition, disease, unsanitary conditions, and endless hours of hard physical labor. Those who became too sick or weak to work were shipped to Buchenwald or Auschwitz and killed.

During the summer months of 1943, Christa worked at the sewing machine factory L.O. Dietrich, according to the paperwork as *kaufm. Angestellte*, a position roughly equivalent to that of a clerk.

I suspect that for Christa the tribulations that came with the impact of living in a country at war and the restrictions on thought and speech in every direction represented obstacles she could absorb and work around while despising them. She hardly needed all her conversations with her father as well as other relatives who were critical of the Nazis to reinforce her personal feelings of horrified disdain. Meanwhile, the woman I knew as my mother was always a master in the art of ignoring things she did not like or could not control, while private about her innermost thoughts. She also was tireless and impervious to discomforts. Ultimately many of the deprivations and obstacles in daily life during the war years had little power over her even if they shaped some of her skills as a consummate survivor.

No, her scars came from the unceasing fear for her brother, her father, and her friends in the field, the increasing realization that the world in which she had grown up was gone for good, and the mood swings of her mother against which Christa had no defense.

Christa came to dread her visits to Altenburg. Both Christa's father and brother would return home for hurried visits when they were on furlough. When Christa's father arrived from the front, Erika was disconcerted because she hadn't expected him and hadn't prepared for his arrival. She fussed and complained that there wasn't enough food or soap, and besides, nothing had been prepared for him.

Bogislav laughed at her. "Look," he said. "I brought plenty of soap." Opening several boxes, he pulled out lavender soap he had purchased while in France as well as all sorts of delicacies such as paté and sardines.

To Christa's intense frustration, Erika insisted on squirreling away most of this manna from heaven and quickly reverted to handing out only the cheap soap produced in Germany during the war. "We need to save the others for when times get worse," she defended herself.

When Bogislav spoke to Christa, he showed his bitterness and his disappointment about such a reception. "Why can't she be happy that I have come home?"

When it came time for him to leave, Erika was upset all over again. She had gotten used to his presence and couldn't adjust to the change. It was as if her feelings of worry about her husband's safety in the field or the grief of being separated from him for an indefinite time were subsumed in her frantic and restless misery at having her daily routines disrupted. Christa felt like a Ping Pong ball batted back and forth between them, her mother fussing and barking at everybody, and her father showing Christa how upset he was at this treatment, especially because he had to return to the front soon.

Hans-Melchior avoided the front door when he arrived home on leave. Instead, at night he tossed pebbles against Christa's window until she woke up. They sat in the cold kitchen talking quietly, while Christa tried to find some food for him. Neither of them wanted to wake up their mother, afraid of the explosion and the fussing.

Christa was always glad to return to university and the relative freedom that it entailed.

❧ 4 ❧

LETTERS FROM THE FIELD

THE FIRST THING CHRISTA DID WHEN BEGINNING HER STUDIES at the University of Leipzig was to cut her hair.

Until 1942, Christa had thick long braids that reached down her back. She had devised a clever method of twisting them around her head so that they stayed up with just a few pins. Her father was furious when Christa told him that the braids were gone. Aside from getting rid of the sheer weight— I speak from experience since I inherited similarly thick hair— it must have been liberating, to say the least.

Her photograph in her university matriculation booklet shows a young woman with pronounced cheekbones and rounded curves, balanced by a strong, slightly hooked nose, with a tentative smile and dreamy eyes. She wore a shirt with a high collar and an elegant overcoat with sharp-cornered lapels, her hair in easy waves just below her chin. The handwriting with its strong, generously shaped, flowing lines on her signature is so familiar it almost hurts to see it.

Given how much was lost during the war, it is remarkable how much of her paperwork from those years Christa managed to keep. In addition to the record of matriculation, I found the student identity number initially assigned to her at the University of Leipzig, No. 271988, which she was to submit for studies at any other university. Other paperwork included the official document indicating that she had completed a medical exam and several certificates attesting to her completion of compulsory labor service. A folded piece of paper in dusky red turned out to be the Certificate of Aryan descent or 'Ancestor Pass.'

The paper used for these documents is thin and brittle, with the brown tinge typical of the times. Paper had become a scarce resource along with other items of daily life.

I know nothing about Christa's time in Leipzig from April until October 1942. I had no idea she studied there until I went through the boxes of files we found after her death.

Leipzig was a city known for its large trade fair, its various industries, especially in textiles, and its music, as well as a history of involvement in liberal movements. The first German labor party, the General German Workers' Association (Allgemeiner Deutscher Arbeiterverein, ADAV) was founded in Leipzig on May 23, 1863.

Its mayor, Carl Friedrich Goerdeler resigned in 1937 after the destruction of the city's statue of Felix Mendelsohn at the instigation of the deputy mayor Hans Rudolf Haake, a committed Nazi. Goerdeler became an active member of the resistance against Hitler and was later executed by the Nazis on February 2, 1945.

The famous synagogue designed by Gottfried Semper had been destroyed during Kristallnacht in 1938. Presumably, Christa saw the carcass of the building.

In 1933, a census recorded that over 11,000 Jews were living in Leipzig. In the 1939 census, the number had fallen to roughly 4,500. In January 1942, the deportations of the remaining 2,000 Jews began. On July 13, 1942, 170 Jews were deported from Leipzig to Auschwitz Concentration Camp, and on September 19, 1942, 440 Jews were deported from Leipzig to Theresienstadt Concentration Camp.

In November 1942, she transferred to the University of Tübingen.

Tübingen is a medieval university town, bisected by the river Neckar and framed by the Swabian Alps. The town is set in hilly terrain, with crooked cobblestone lanes, narrow-stair alleyways, streets lined with canals, and traditional half-timbered houses. It was home to the philosopher Hegel and the poet of Romanticism Friedrich Hölderlin, to name a few of the notable people of the town.

Christa loved everything about Tübingen, reveling in its cultural attractions, the churches, and her lectures at the art institute. To her amusement, one of her professors impressed everyone not only with the range of his knowledge but his ability to start an extremely long and convoluted sentence about a complex subject and elegantly bring the sentence and the day's lecture to its conclusion precisely at the ringing of the bell.

Christa arrived in Tübingen in late October. For a brief time, she kept a journal. Two years later, in October 1944, she felt compelled to write down some of her experiences in a retrospective account in this same journal. There are no other journals—and no entries about Leipzig or Prague. One of the first entries in the journal states, "This is the day when Heinrich arrives."

Heinrich Hartmann was a navy medic-midshipman (*Marine-Sanitäts-Oberfähnrich*) and was studying for his medical degree. As far as I can piece things together, Christa and Heinrich had met in Leipzig. He was matriculated at the University of Tübingen, and during the winter semester 1942-1943, they spent a great deal of time together. Subsequently, he started his navy training and would see Christa only during holidays. He introduced Christa to some of his professors and told her about the various courses in medicine that he had taken.

The papers I found after Christa's death include a book

box filled with letters from Heinrich. The sheer volume is breathtaking—seven thick binders, meticulously arranged, and four booklets, all filled with letters. It is as if he wrote to Christa every single day from the time that they first met, sometime in the spring of 1942 until November 1944.

The binders are lovingly decorated with postcards of works of art, churches, and other notable pieces of architecture, poems copied out of books, flowers pressed into the pages, and sketches. Heinrich's handwriting is unforgettable— dense, tight, precise, with sharply drawn letters, in regular lines on unlined paper. Many letters are written on thin and fragile paper, with the ink fading after all this time. Where Heinrich used pencil, the script is almost completely worn away.

I also found a small booklet, entitled *A Contract of Marriage between Ferdinand and Louise*, with a dedication card "To my dear Christa, June 26, 1942."

It contains Articles 1-10 of basic tenets of what would make a good marriage and what the expectations of the partners would be. Thus, for instance, article 3 decrees that Louise would dedicate herself to keeping the house and daily life in good order while preventing excesses. Article 4 advises the partners to let go of small disagreements. It advises against adornments and jewelry, arguing that those might give the impression that Louise would want to attract other men. According to Article 7, Louise should never show any disrespect to her husband in public, while Article 8 decrees that Ferdinand will publicly honor Louise and not allow any other women to triumph over her.

Reading this in the year 2020, I found the earnest, moralizing tone funny and had a hard time seeing Christa in this context. Her relationship with my father was a universe away from this sort of thinking.

At social events, Christa and Wolf Ulrich drew each other's attention to people whom they considered attractive. "I think you might like him," he would whisper into Christa's ear. "Check him out." Driving around in Rome during the first years of their marriage, Wolf Ulrich would step on the brakes when he saw an appealing woman crossing the street. Craning his head back to catch another glimpse, he would say, "Should I stop?" Christa laughed, while calmly suggesting he better keep driving if he didn't want to cause a traffic jam.

Christa's journal of her time in Tübingen includes a series of black and white photographs, mostly portrait shots, with and without a headscarf, her hair hanging loose down to her shoulders. In many of them, she smiles, shy, not entirely comfortable in front of the camera, and yet completely recognizable as the woman she was to become—elegant, stubborn, intensely private, and with a fundamental serenity that never quite left her, even during the worst of times.

Portrait shots of Heinrich show a pleasant-looking man, with a round face and dark eyes, serious and absurdly young. He strikes me as somewhat stiff, straitlaced, and fastidious.

It is entirely presumptuous of me to arrive at any conclusions about this man—in truth, I know very little about him. From the few comments by Christa and the impression one gets from his letters, he must have been a gentle, considerate, and thoughtful person, and deeply in love with Christa. Unquestionably Heinrich occupied a central place in Christa's life during those years.

Not only did he write every day, but he visited as often as he could. He would whistle outside of her window at the house where she rented a room, always bearing a gift—flowers, food, chocolates, a book, or a poem. They went for long walks all over Tübingen and took the car to visit various points of interest in the region.

Heinrich was a Catholic. They attended Mass together, and in her journal, Christa mentions "long serious conversations." In later years, my mother sometimes told me that she almost converted to Catholicism at one time in her life and always continued to feel a lingering attraction to it; however, she never said anything about Heinrich.

In his letters, Heinrich comes across as mystical at times, steeped in faith, quoting scripture, and including many postcards with religious themes. His letters are a testament to a desperate need to escape onto another plane of being—an inner world untouched by what was happening, a world of art, philosophy, and faith.

While in Tübingen, Christa's art history studies focused on Tilman Riemenschneider, a 15th-century German sculptor, woodcarver, and renowned master in stone and limewood. He produced pieces for churches, including entire altarpieces and sculptures for tombs. He created wooden sculptures with a variety of religious themes and unforgettable faces of men and women of various ages. They are expressive and moving, with sad heavy eyes and deeply etched lines of sorrow and suffering.

In my mind, Christa's fascination with Riemenschneider's work—stark, austere, and uncompromising—presented a curious echo of her relationship with Heinrich.

Occasionally, Heinrich descended to a more human plane when talking about the great pressure experienced by him and his comrades in the field. He even voiced a gentle complaint about not receiving more mail from Christa and argued that she could not begin to understand what it was like in the field. At other times he provided descriptions of his work as a medic and doctor and the pleasure he derived from it. Letters veered from the philosophical and mystical to the practical, thus proudly telling Christa that he managed to buy three pieces of underwear and that his new uniform had arrived.

For Christa, Heinrich's intense focus on her must have been a bewitching experience. At home, she was the peacemaker, the person to whom no one paid much attention, the reliable one, while her brother leaped from one disaster into the next. She once said, "Hans-Melchior was thrown out of so many schools that I lost count." For Christa, with the echo of her father's high expectations and the bark and bite of her mother's volatile temper in her mind, spending time with Heinrich must have been like being wrapped in a warm, soft blanket.

In her journal, Christa indicated that some of her friends and professors in Tübingen knew of her involvement with Heinrich and were supportive. Reading between the lines, I concluded that Christa was the recipient of a lot of negative comments from her mother and perhaps other family members about this relationship. Did Christa's father know about Heinrich? I suspect not.

Perhaps her mother objected to Heinrich's middle-class background or his Catholicism. She could hardly have objected on the grounds that Christa was too young; Erika herself had married when she was nineteen.

Christa talked about how kind and truly good Heinrich was. My more cynical self thinks that she loved her newfound freedom, away from her father's high expectations and her mother's temper, life in the university town, and the world of art as much as she was in love with Heinrich.

In the middle of the winter semester in Tübingen, Christa received the news of the death of her father and her brother. Hans-Melchior lost his life on January 10, 1943 in the southern part of Ukraine, near Rostov-on-Don, Soviet Union. Her father was killed on January 13, 1943 near Larissa, Greece. He died in what was described as an accident; it involved an empty train traveling on the same track as my grandfather's military command train which resulted in a frontal collision. The foreign press, including a *New York Times* article on January 24, 1943, questioned the Nazi report of the so-called "accident," deeming Bogislav von Studnitz's death suspicious.

Christa was convinced that her father had been murdered. As a general who commanded loyalty among his troops and was opposed to the Nazi regime, he was feared as a potential member of the active resistance. In lieu of a funeral, since his remains were interred in Greece, a service was held in Buderose, Pomerania, where Bogislav was born. Hitler had sent a wreath. My mother told me that the temptation to toss the wreath onto the nearest compost heap was hard to resist.

In her journal, Christa referred to her father's and her brother's death only by pitying the young woman who had to convey the news to her. She never put down anything else in writing. She did not talk to us about what it was like to receive the news of her brother's and father's death. Only once, she told me that throughout all the years of her childhood she had always known when something was wrong with her brother. "I knew he was gone even before I got the news."

Her friend Ursula, who had known Hans-Melchior and had some romantic feelings towards him, told me that Christa came home for a couple of days and then returned directly to Tübingen. At the time, Ursula was upset and hurt; it seemed to her that Christa was placing her love for Heinrich over her feelings for Hans-Melchior and her father.

It was Christa's modus vivendi. When confronted with something as overwhelming as the loss of her beloved father and brother, she shut down. It did not surprise me in the least that she could not put any of her thoughts to paper or that she did not want to spend more time with her mother in Altenburg when she had an escape route available to her.

Throughout my childhood, the month of January presented a major hurdle in the year. My mother suffered from debilitating migraines, and, invariably during the first weeks of January, she would spend several days in a darkened room, not eating anything. When the migraine passed and the calendar moved forward, she would emerge, shaken and quiet but willing to return to the world of the living. Meanwhile, she never spoke about the significance of those dates, and it wasn't until later that I was able to piece things together.

"Our mother is going to run out of months soon," Adrian joked several years before her death. Whenever someone close to Christa died, the date of death became enshrined in her soul and was commemorated with long-lasting migraines. Meanwhile, outwardly she was always composed and calm when confronted with bad news.

An officer notified Erika of the death of her husband. A couple of days later, when the news of Hans-Melchior's death had come through, another officer embarked on the journey to her house to bring her the news. When he walked in, he found her dressed in mourning. Shocked, he blurted out, "You have already heard the news?"

"Yes," Erika said. "Thank you for coming. I have heard about my husband."

The officer started to stammer. At this point, she realized that the officer wasn't talking about Bogislav but instead Hans-Melchior.

The officer was so shaken that Erika gave him a glass of cognac and tried to console him for having to bring her the news of her son's death.

In situations like this, Erika was invincible. It illustrates a demeanor under pressure that was drummed into us throughout our childhood. *Haltung,* translated as posture, with the implied notion of maintaining one's composure and not falling apart—was valued by my parents and many members of their generation and upbringing, and as we grew up, we saw many instances of this.

In the spring of 1943, Christa left Tübingen to return to Leipzig for a semester.

Christa met Egloff von Tippelskirch during a visit home.

In many respects, Egloff's background as a descendant of a family with roots in the Baltic, Prussia, and Silesia dating back to the 12th century, steeped in the Protestant work ethic in the best sense of the term, and a history of service, in particular, in the military, must have resonated with Christa.

His father and his two brothers served in the military. Egloff's uncle, Kurt von Tippelskirch, owner of an estate in Silesia near Wroclaw, had no children. In order to keep the estate in the family, Kurt adopted Egloff when he was already an adult. His adoptive mother, né Elisabeth von Knobelsdorff, was an architect and one of the first women to earn a degree in engineering, with a distinguished career including an appointment as a master builder for the government in Germany in 1921. She worked as an architect in Berlin-Charlottenburg until she accompanied her husband to the United States in 1927. Egloff's adoptive father had a career in the Foreign Office.

Egloff, born in 1913, was a lawyer by training. He studied at the Universities of Berlin and Freiburg. In the course of his studies, he also spent time in England and at Dickinson College in Carlisle, Pennsylvania under the auspices of the Institute of International Education, where he focused on American criminal law and history and received a degree with the class of 1933. The Dickinson College Archives and Special Collections Department has a moving "In Remembrance" section dedicated to students who lost their lives in various wars. In the long list of students who did not return from World War II, there is an entry for Egloff, who is described as "a tall and unassuming boy." Once he returned to Berlin, he continued his studies and ultimately earned his doctorate.

Thus, Egloff come from the same social circle and class as Christa, and he also had exposure to the world beyond Germany. They spoke the same language, to use a trite term, and shared the same set of values. His international outlook and perspective as a result of his studies abroad, combined with his pragmatism and clear-headed determination, were powerful magnets for Christa.

Egloff met Christa at a party hosted by a mutual friend. After this introduction, Egloff wrote to Christa, addressing her by her last name and *Sie*, correct and formal, meanwhile specifying exactly when and where she was to meet him on his way back to the front via Leipzig. This was the beginning of the siege—in the form of countless letters. He was determined to marry Christa.

In the subsequent letters, the formality lessened. In his letters, Egloff comes across as liberal in his thinking and willing to ignore conventional thinking and attitudes, but at the same time autocratic and relentless in his demeanor and his convictions.

My brothers and I sometimes speculated about what our lives would have been like if we had ended up with Egloff as a parent and decided that we had not fared all that badly with our father.

When they waited in line somewhere, for instance, for tickets to the theater, Egloff insisted that they use the time by memorizing and reciting poetry. He also introduced her to the saying, "Whoever feels cold is either stupid or a soldier." The translation of this was that a soldier had no choice and had to freeze, while anyone else had a choice and in Egloff's words could "choose to carry a heavy block of wood around the room until warmed up."

This convinced Christa that Egloff would survive and thrive in whatever situation life would land him in. It struck her as an attractive quality in a time when her entire world appeared to be collapsing all around her.

Christa told Egloff about Heinrich and that she had been in the process of breaking off her relationship but had resumed it again. Egloff was not deterred by this in the least. He discussed Christa's hesitations, dismissed them, and laid out in no uncertain terms how they would be perfect together. He left no doubt about his feelings, and his complete conviction about the rightness of it all leaves the impression of being overrun by a steamroller. He repeatedly argued that for Christa to decide out of a feeling of guilt would be detrimental to all parties concerned.

In contrast, Heinrich's letters convey the impression of a dreamer and idealist, while also firmly rooted in conventional thinking of the times.

What attracted Egloff and Heinrich to Christa? She was an appealing, profoundly feminine young woman, with much going for her in terms of her interests and passions. Meanwhile, I think that the main point of attraction lay in her ability to be happy regardless of circumstances.

"You have to be able to enjoy the little pleasures," she always told me.

One of her favorite songs, "Go forth, my heart and seek delight," defined Christa's approach to whatever the day offered. If anyone should know the meaning of resilience, it would be Paul Gerhardt who wrote the lyrics for this hymn just five years after the end of the Thirty Years War.

Go forth, my heart, and seek delight
In all the gifts of God's great might,
These pleasant summer hours:
Look how the plains for thee and me
Have decked themselves most fair to see,
All bright and sweet with flowers.

For Christa, little pleasures were infinite—blue cornflowers along the side of the road, crunchy sugar on top of a plum cake, watching glowing embers in a fireplace. I still see her in my mind running her fork through a dish of mashed potatoes, looking utterly satisfied and content with life. When she talked about something that intrigued her, her animation was bewitching. She glowed.

Her vivid intelligence and interest in everything around her, together with her capacity for joy must have been irresistible for friends and these men in particular, especially at a time when everyone was desperately trying to hold on to a semblance of normality and a sense of hope for the life to come.

Meanwhile, given the benefit of having known the woman Christa would become—determined, decisive, and strong-willed, anything but compliant or submissive—I struggled to imagine her in the context of her relationships with both Heinrich and Egloff.

Yet, when I thought about it more, it began to make sense.

Of course, one must not reduce what happened to the natural progression of one first love affair giving way to a second one.

Christa was barely nineteen when she met Heinrich and embarked on what was her first serious relationship.

Sitting in front of the piles of letters from Heinrich and Egloff, I felt tremendous pity for Christa. She was living through an unceasing barrage of letters from men who considered her the source and central point of a future life, clinging to her, while serving at the front or in various officer training activities. Every day she heard of the death of one or another of her friends or relatives. Her sense of guilt and her fear to write a letter breaking off a relationship for good must have been agonizing.

At the same time, the letters provided a source of respite from the unceasing drabness of war times, with occasional packages of food and reading material as diversions. Letters provided some news even if the conveyance of news was circumscribed, as well as a source of entertainment, warmth, and affection.

For Christa, writing letters represented an escape of sorts while offering an elegant way for hiding some of her thoughts behind a wealth of information as well as interest in another's life. Heinrich repeatedly complained that he felt she was evading his questions.

In a letter to a friend, Christa pointed out that Egloff taught her to laugh again. From the sparse comments in her journal and the letters from Heinrich, I got the impression that Christa's relationship with Heinrich was more staid and serious, with little laughter.

Egloff responded to some of her fears about marriage as something confining and limiting; she had apparently written about these in her letters. Christa wanted to make a life for herself, especially now that she had found a field of study that she loved. Egloff repeatedly assured her that the last thing he wanted to do was to confine her in any way and to hinder her from pursuing her passions. "You told me your doubts about marriage to Heinrich are based on "superficial factors," but you don't elaborate," Egloff complained, evidently unsatisfied with her arguments. I suspect that they pertained to her doubts about entering another social milieu, something she found hard to express, especially since she may have been unsure of her reasoning and mistrusted her motivation.

Egloff firmly dismissed this reasoning. "Either you love this man, or you don't; any superficial factors, whatever those may be, are irrelevant." He essentially told her that she had to "fish or cut bait," and that any man would prefer to know and have clarity rather than to be waiting in agony for a decision. "But you need to decide. Any commitment from you has to be complete and unequivocal."

Christa put off making a decision. Instead, in the late fall of 1943, she applied for and was granted a transfer to study at the art institute of the German University in Prague.

5

THE GOLDEN CITY

In a letter to a friend, Christa described her plan to study in Prague as a *Flucht nach vorne*, an escape forward.

Flucht nach vorne is a military expression referring to a reaction when one cannot withstand the pressure one has come under and chooses to take the initiative, charging headlong into enemy fire. It was a fitting description. Christa rebelled against the accepted norms of behavior for young women of marriageable age that had been drummed into her willy-nilly in the form of outright Nazi propaganda as well as general societal expectations. Struggling with her grief over the loss of her father and brother, she was caught between Heinrich and Egloff and could not see any way out of her dilemma. A few semesters in Prague promised to provide a welcome respite from some of these pressures. At the same time, she had discovered a genuine passion for the field of art history and was determined to build the foundation for a career of her own. It partially explains the curious disconnect between Christa's glowing recollections of her time in the fabled "Golden City" and the reality of the historical context.

Christa's matriculation document from the German University of Prague is dated December 13, 1943. By the time

Christa arrived in Prague, the Czech people had been living under Nazi occupation since 1939.

In the fall of 1938, Hitler's army had taken control of the Sudetenland border region of Czechoslovakia under the guise of "liberating" the German population in that area. This was the beginning of an invasion that led to the occupation of Prague in 1939, the declaration of a German Protectorate of Bohemia and Moravia, and the eventual establishment of the concentration camp in Theresienstadt. The eventual goal of the Germanization of the annexed territories involved assimilation, deportation, and extermination of Czechs in general and Jews in particular. In Bohemia and Moravia, the Jewish population, numbering around 118,000, was essentially wiped out. Some managed to emigrate after 1939; over 70,000 lost their lives in the concentration camps.

For the most part, the Czech population capitulated and hunkered down, quietly accepting the new state of affairs. In the subsequent years, efforts at expressions of Czech nationality and resistance to the occupation were ruthlessly suppressed. Meanwhile, the slowly emerging resistance was itself splintered into numerous groups with conflicting goals and motivations. Some efforts, for instance, the assassination of Reinhard Heydrich in 1942, led to unspeakably brutal repercussions, mass arrests, executions, and the outright slaughter of the villages of Lidice and Ležáky in their entirety.

The University of Prague was founded in 1348. Its history as one of the oldest universities in Europe in continuous operation is a microcosm of the history of Prague. The Thirty Years War was reflected in the struggles between the Hussites and the Jesuits over control of the university, just as the revolution of 1848 energized the struggles between Czech speaking professors and students and German-speaking professors and students, ultimately leading to the split of the university into two institutions, the German University and the Czech University in 1882.

In 1939, the Nazis closed the Czech University and all other Czech institutions of higher learning as part of their asserting control over the population; they followed up with persecutions of students and professors. These institutions remained closed until the end of World War II. Nine student leaders were executed and about 1,200 Czech students were interned in Sachsenhausen and not released until 1943, with at least twenty students losing their lives while interned. This marked the end of the coexistence of the two universities. The German University continued to operate until 1945 after which it ceased to exist.

In the war years, the university struggled to survive and for that reason welcomed students with open arms. For that reason, Christa had no difficulty when she applied for permission to transfer from the university in Tübingen.

By 1944, most museums and all theatres were closed. Many stores were empty, and streets were littered with garbage. Blackouts and rationing were factors of daily life as was the presence of SS guards throughout the city.

Christa never talked about any of that. She loved to show me her books about Prague, including the spectacular collection of images of Prague photographed by the Czechoslovak photographer, film director, and cinematographer Karel Plicka. Once, when I was preparing for a brief trip to Prague, Christa sat me down and instructed me on all the important sights I should not miss under any circumstances. "If you don't see these things when you go, I will send you straight back," she said with the passionate intensity I loved about her, her eyes brilliant and her face shining with enthusiasm.

She fell in love with the "City of a Hundred Spires," enchanted by its bridges over the Vltava and the endless palaces, churches, and gardens. For a young student of art history, Prague must have been a veritable treasure trove. More than any other city in Europe, Prague stands out for seamlessly blending different architectural styles through the centuries from the Romanesque and Gothic to the Renaissance, the Baroque, Classicism, Art Nouveau, and Cubism to name just a few.

Maria Wellershoff, a close friend of Christa's, wrote a book about her childhood and her years as a student during World War II entitled *Von Ort zu Ort: Eine Jugend in Pommern* (From Village to Village: Growing up in Pomerania). Her descriptions included glimpses of Christa's life in Prague.

The two young women shared a room in a student dormitory. Students preferred staying in such a dormitory instead of renting a room from a Czech resident. Such an arrangement could become uncomfortable for both parties as it became increasingly apparent that the war would end in a defeat for Germany. Prague residents were reserved with the German students but generally did not show any open hostility.

Sitting in a cubicle next to the entrance of the dormitory, a *domovnik* (custodian) guarded the building, ostensibly to prevent access to any unannounced individuals, in particular, men. Nonetheless one ran into men in the mornings in the hallway or on the way to the common bathroom on the floor, watching them quietly slip out, carrying their shoes in their hands. Everybody pretended not to have noticed anything. The residents of the dormitory shared a common kitchen area. Each room contained two beds, a cabinet, a bench with storage underneath, a table, and a couple of chairs.

Maria claimed that once Christa moved in, their room quickly became more habitable and attractive. This struck me as familiar. Wherever I spent time with my mother, she added her personal note to the space, even if it was merely a shabby motel room—merely by arranging her things neatly, spreading a piece of fabric over a dresser, or filling a jam jar with flowers. Maria was proud that she and Christa never argued despite the confined space.

Christa and Maria, both trained from childhood on to be frugal, had no problem in living modestly. Meanwhile, this did not hinder them from inviting people for dinner. Usually, Christa cooked such meals in the common kitchen of the building since they both accepted that she was the better cook of the two. In the evenings they sometimes sat together to darn their stockings. When there were runs in the silk hose, they glued the ends with clear nail polish. Stockings were rationed, and they had to make do with what they had for as long as possible.

The students at the art institute studied hard. They spent most of the time in the library, bent silently over their papers. Christa saved a booklet crammed with notes about various lectures from her time in Prague. She studied the history of ancient art and architecture, Gottfried Semper who designed among others the famous Semper Synagogue in Dresden, destroyed during Kristallnacht in 1938, the art of painting under glass, and the 18th-century painter Daniel Chodowiecki, to name a few. Bizarrely, the booklet has Heinrich's name printed on the front. Perhaps, it was one of his gifts to Christa, since paper was so hard to come by. Christa's handwriting is unmistakable, and the notes give the impression of a student completely immersed in the subject matter.

The general sense of oppression and doom did not keep Christa and her close friends from enjoying their time for all that they knew it was life in a bubble, soon to come to an end. Once, Christa helped the others to bend down a branch of a cherry tree that stretched across the fence so that they could reach the sweet cherries. They ate lunch in one of the large restaurants near the Rudolfinum, feasting on *Knödel* (in Czech *knedlik*)—potato-dough dumplings, *Buchteln* (in Czech *buchta*)— sweet rolls made of yeast dough, filled with jam, ground poppy seeds, or curd, and *Palatschinken*—thin pancakes similar to the French crêpe, rolled with apricot, strawberry, or plum jam, and sprinkled with confectioner's sugar.

Christa made many of these recipes for us when we were growing up. My favorite was *Kaiserschmarren*, a light, caramelized pancake made from a sweet batter using flour, eggs, sugar, salt, and milk, baked in butter, and served hot with apple or plum sauce.

Completing the image of perverse normalcy, upper-class society life in Prague continued unabated despite the inescapable reality of life under Nazi rule. Christa, thanks to her family's international contacts and familial connections and her father's position as military attaché, knew several prominent Czech families of the nobility in Prague. Christa took Maria along to events in imposing palaces and mansions throughout Prague. In her book, Maria mentions names such as Czernin, Lobkowitz, and Dubsky, all previously unknown to her. Meanwhile, Christa moved about in this society with a self-assurance that was astounding to Maria.

Maria pointed out that there were very few students with whom one could talk openly. The only ones she trusted were Christa and Barbara Reuter, who was to become a lifelong friend as well as my godmother.

Maria's half-sister, Elisabeth von Thadden, a member of the Solf Circle, a resistance group against Hitler, had been arrested on January 12, 1944. She was subjected to months of dreadful treatment and lengthy interrogations in various prisons and the penal bunker at the Ravensbrück concentration camp. Maria repeatedly tried to see Elisabeth, but her sister refused her visits because she did not want Maria to see the condition she was in. On 1 July 1944, the *Volksgerichtshof*, the so-called People's Court presided over by Roland Freisler, sentenced Elisabeth von Thadden to death for conspiring to commit high treason and undermining the fighting forces (*Wehrkraftzersetzung*). Ten weeks later, on September 8, 1944, she was beheaded at Plötzensee Prison.

Maria could not remember whether she and Christa talked about the assassination attempt on July 20, 1944. However, they both personally knew several people involved in the resistance.

Christa's uncle Friedrich von Zitzewitz, the last owner of Muttrin, was arrested after the July 20, 1944 attempt to assassinate Hitler because of his association with the so-called Reusch-Kreis, a discussion group of six landowners and six industrialists and in close contact with the resistance group around Carl Goerdeler. The Gestapo also arrested twelve other Pomeranian estate owners who had been part of the resistance. One of these, Malte von Veltheim Fürst zu Putbus, died in a concentration camp, while Alexander von Kameke and Oscar Caminecci-Zettuhn were both executed. Friedrich von Zitzewitz was tried by the People's Court under Roland Freisler in January 1945 and sentenced to prison. He only regained his freedom at the end of World War II and the arrival of the US army.

Maria and another friend went on an excursion outside of Prague. On the return trip, picked up by a chauffeur, they drove past the concentration camp Theresienstadt, where large road signs indicated a minimum speed of sixty kilometers for through traffic. It was clear to Maria that this was to prevent passengers from being able to see too much from the road. However, they could make out the buildings and at one point a long line of inmates, with shaved heads, black-and-white striped pants and tops, and wooden clogs. Heavily armed guards with German shepherds escorted them along the other side of the road. In her journal, Maria only noted that she and her friend were silent on the way home, in part because they were nervous about talking in front of the chauffeur.

Maria cited the motto that circulated among Germans in those years, *Geniesst den Krieg, der Frieden wird fürchterlich*! "Enjoy the war; peace will be horrific." This motto reflected two possible alternatives. If Germany lost, as Christa and her friends hoped, the Allied Powers would dictate the terms of the peace, punishing the Germans and dismantling all industry, Germany would turn into a farming community, and all universities would be closed indefinitely. The second alternative, increasingly unlikely, was that the Nazis would prevail and then continue their inhuman, contemptuous, racist, and anti-cultural ideology, and everything would be even worse.

Thus, inspired not to waste a single good moment, everyone followed the motto *carpe diem* while praying the Western Allies would successfully invade Normandy. Maria called it "Dancing on top of a volcano."

Friendships with soldiers were tinged with the painful awareness of their uncertain future.

One of Christa's satellites, as her friend Maria described him, visited regularly; Harald von Kügelgen liked to engage Maria and Christa in serious discussions and philosophical musings and took them out to feast on *knedlik* and *palatschinken*. When Christa was away, he would take Maria for walks as a substitute. This friend survived the war, although he was badly wounded. I remember a tall man with a bad limp who would sometimes come to visit my parents when we lived in Germany.

Christa's dissertation advisor at the university was Karl Maria Swoboda, of Czech and Austrian descent. He was fluent in both German and Czech and was appointed to a lectureship at the University of Prague in 1934. His first marriage to Kamilla Rabl ended in divorce in 1934. Swoboda's second wife, Hermine Hein, was concerned about the safety of Kamilla who was Jewish. She tried to convince Kamilla to emigrate, in particular, since her son was already abroad. However, Kamilla declined and was deported to Theresienstadt in 1942 and from there to Lublin.

In May 1945, Swoboda was arrested by the Soviet authorities and accused of having been a Nazi sympathizer. However, his Czech colleagues obtained his release, arguing that he had been an opponent of National Socialism while teaching in Prague and had frequently used his connections to help Czech nationals threatened by the regime. In 1946,

Swoboda went to Vienna where he taught at the Wiener Lehrkanzel. He continued to live in Austria until he died in 1977.

He was famous for his haughtiness, high expectations, and ruthless criticism of his students. Christa claimed that once, when presented by one of his students with her dissertation, he said, "This is a good start, my dear. Now I suggest you begin with the second half."

Christa's dissertation topic was the German portrait painter Franz Gerhard von Kügelgen (1772-1820). Kügelgen was noted for his portraits and history paintings. During his career, he painted portraits of Caspar David Friedrich, Johann Wolfgang von Goethe, Johann Gottfried Herder, August von Kotzebue, Friedrich Schiller, Johann Gottfried Seume, Ludwig Uhland, Zacharias Werner, Christoph Martin Wieland, Johann Carl Simon Morgenstern, and other writers, artists, and scholars of his time as well as numerous members of the Russian nobility, the tsar, and his family. His works can be found in Russia, Germany, Latvia, and Estonia, among others.

One of his paintings, the *Madonna of the Veil*, belonged to Christa's mother. It is a luminous portrait of a woman filled with sorrow and pain, so exquisite in its detail that you believe you can breathe the scent from her soft skin. The painting represents a fascinating blend of artistic periods. Kügelgen was inspired by Carlo Dolci, a 17th-century painter of devotional pieces that convey an idealized version of piety. At the same time, Kügelgen was firmly rooted in the school of portraiture during the age of Romanticism, with its focus on the individual and the expression of a wide range of psychological and emotional states.

Thus, Christa traveled from the austere wooden sculptures of Tilman Riemenschneider in the 15th century, with their unbending religious symbolism, to the luminous portraits of a painter associated with the age of early romanticism.

Of course, it is superficial to see this progression from

Riemenschneider to Kügelgen as a reflection of Christa's personal trajectory and yet tempting as well. Her relationship with Heinrich represented a venture into unfamiliar territory, steeped in idealism and mysticism as well as an embrace of Catholicism.

The painter Kügelgen represented a link to a world Christa knew. Her best friend from school was a distant relative of the painter, and another friend, Harald von Kügelgen, was a direct descendant. Both the realism in the painter's portraits as well as his eclectic flexibility in drawing on various schools of art may have appealed to Christa, ready to move beyond the austere purity of Riemenschneider.

Egloff's world was one that Christa recognized and embraced. Furthermore, his pragmatic approach to life and his open-mindedness may have done much to remove her concerns about marriage as confining and limiting.

Meanwhile, Christa kept putting him off, refusing to make a decision.

On July 18, 1944, Christa received a notification from the *Reichsstudentenführung*, notifying her about her work assignment at the Institute of Art. The *Reichsstudentenführung* was an administrative body directly governed by the National Socialist Party and in charge of all matters concerning students at all institutes of higher learning, including the compulsory Reich Labor Service (RAD). This work assignment came about as a result of her professor's efforts.

Professor Swoboda tried to find comfortable and innocuous assignments for his students who had to comply with the work requirements imposed by the RAD. Thus, he arranged that some of the young art history students could spend time in one or another castle in the vicinity, ostensibly to draw up inventories of works of art on private estates that had been seized by the Nazis. Maria questioned this activity in light of the irony of preparing inventories for a regime that was likely to come to a bitter end while appreciating Swoboda's thoughtfulness in arranging the work. It afforded the students with a reasonably safe environment while possibly, in the best-case scenario, providing the unfortunate owners with such inventories. Certainly, it was vastly preferable to working in an armaments factory. In one of his letters, Egloff wrote that he was imagining Christa in her "castle." So, she must have spent some time drawing up such inventories.

The first air raid warning in Prague toward the end of July coincided with the end of the semester. According to Maria, Prague residents were shocked. They hadn't expected this, and the result was major confusion and helplessness. Maria and Christa were less impressed.

This same nonchalant attitude is reflected in a letter to Egloff, returned to her after Egloff's death. Christa made a wry comment about air raids as "background music, with occasional *Husarenstreiche* by pilots of attacking aircraft thrown into the mix." *Husarenstreich*, a term from the 17th century, refers to hussars (light cavalry) engaged in a crazy, foolhardy venture or daring coup.

Christa's wry tone was typical of how my parents and others from their generation spoke, with an emphasis on understatement. It also reflected how many people tended to speak about events during the war. An ironic and laconic form of self-expression was a way to protect oneself from being overwhelmed and helped to maintain some sort of emotional control while presenting the least burden for another person listening to you or reading your words.

Around this time, in a letter to Christa, Egloff reported the death of one of his brothers on the front and the news that another brother was missing in action and presumed dead as well. His words were terse and matter-of-fact. "I don't need to tell you how this feels," he said. It was yet another factor bringing them closer together.

There are no letters from Christa to Egloff or Heinrich, with one exception each. One letter to Heinrich was returned to her by Heinrich's mother. Christa wrote to Heinrich during a brief trip to Vienna in the summer of 1944, describing her impressions of the city. It reads like a breezy tourist's report, devoid of any more personal comments as if she was beginning to withdraw from the relationship but didn't yet have the nerve to say so openly.

Meanwhile, life was getting progressively difficult. In the late summer of 1944, Christa left Prague and returned home to Altenburg. In one of his letters to Christa in the fall of 1944, Egloff expresses his dismay that she should still be forced to continue with her factory work. Perhaps she worked at HASAG again, even though she had already completed several periods of work there in 1942 and 1943, but I have no record of this. He commented on her cheerful attitude and expressed his concern that she would not have enough food to eat.

She wrote back to reassure him that she and her mother still had a supply of potatoes and that unless they were forced to surrender a portion of this during a levy, they would not starve for the time being.

In October 1944, Christa wrote her retrospective account of her time in Tübingen, trying to describe everything "as long as my memory is still clear." Christa talked about how this time would never come back and how she hoped that she might be able to revive some of it at a later date. It appeared that in her mind she was already saying goodbye to those years and to Heinrich. "Today Heinrich is going to board his ship, and now his life is in God's hands."

At that time, Christa must have decided to cut the Gordian knot by writing to both Heinrich and Egloff. In November, Egloff wrote to Christa, telling her how happy he was about being engaged to her. He also talked about writing to Christa's mother to obtain her consent.

During those same weeks, Heinrich sent several letters in which he bemoaned the fact that he hadn't received any letters from Christa for a while. He wrote about his hopes for the future marriage, talked about the life to come, the process of rebuilding when nothing was left, the children he hoped for, and the love and faith that kept everything together. He wondered about Christa's silence and earnestly affirmed his belief in her. It was the saddest thing to read.

Heinrich was killed in action on December 9, 1944.

A notice of Christa's engagement appeared on December 19, 1944.

Shortly after Christa's twenty-first birthday, on December 28, 1944, Christa and Egloff got married on the estate Egloff would inherit from his adoptive father in Jakobsdorf, Silesia, today Jagodnik near Wroclaw. On the day of the wedding, Christa was weak from anemia-induced jaundice and also afflicted with a tremendous head cold.

They spent a few weeks together while Egloff was on leave. He returned to the field, and Christa joined her mother in Altenburg.

❧ 6 ☙

WAITING

BEETS. MASHED, BOILED, ROASTED. BEETS IN BREAD, BEETS IN soup, beets plain. Pickled beets. Beet jam. Beet juice. Beets for breakfast, beets for lunch, beets for dinner. Sweeter and more cloying with every meal, and the distinctive earthy taste evoking thoughts of things rotting in the ground.

During the last years of World War II, and in the aftermath, that humble root vegetable was one of the few food items more readily available.

In my recollection, it was as if all of Christa's stories about Altenburg acquired some of the dark red stain of beets, overlaid by the miasma of Erika's depression. Many years later, my mother would still shudder when confronted with the distinctive red slices. Beets were never allowed in our house when I was growing up. I internalized Christa's complete aversion to beets to the point that I avoided them myself for years.

Life shrank to a stubborn battle against constant hunger and the relentless cold that seeped into everything. Christa had an enamel wash bowl and water pitcher on the dresser in her room. Often the water in the pitcher was frozen when she woke up in the morning.

Egloff, whom Christa described as someone rather free

with advice, had told Christa, "If you are cold, take a heavy piece of wood and carry it around in your room for a while, until you have warmed up." Apparently, his own advice didn't help him all that much anymore. "It's very cold," Egloff wrote in February 1945. "There is no heat in the barracks. I am sitting in my fur coat, remembering how I used to say that whether one is cold or not is a question of willpower."

In Altenburg, Christa and her mother were still living in the apartment building at Bismarckstrasse 2. During the war, maintenance jobs in the common areas of the building were divided up among the residents to institute a semblance of order. Thus, they took turns cleaning the large central staircase. Erika had already begun to assume the grim mantle of dutiful compliance with rules and regulations that became a mask to conceal any emotions of loss or grief in later years. When it was her turn, she insisted on doing the work immediately.

"Why waste energy?" Christa said. "The building might be bombed this week." She put it off until the very last minute. As it turned out, Altenburg did not suffer major damage during World War II, even though it experienced at least 260 air raids.

In those years, Erika, for all that she was indomitable in emergencies, was frequently depressed in day-to-day life. Sometimes Christa was afraid to walk into the rooms they shared; the very air was thick with the stifling fog of her gloom.

My grandmother spent much of her time knitting. The products of her labor helped to supply refugees from all points east and those who had lost their housing as a result of bomb attacks with warm hats, sweaters, and gloves. She continued to knit throughout my childhood. Restlessly clicking her needles and only pausing to smoke, she always gave the impression of suppressed nervous energy and unhappiness. Oddly enough, when my mother was knitting, I felt it a source of comfort. I loved to watch her contentedly counting the stitches and purls and laughing when she had to redo an entire row.

The end of the war arrived with a whimper; there was no rejoicing. The US Army reached Altenburg on April 15, 1945, entering the city without any struggle. It was replaced by the Soviet Army on July 1, 1945.

The only immediate result was that initially there were no ration cards at all, and everything came to a stop for residents already weary from months and years of struggling to survive. Most stockpiles built up during the war had been depleted. Agriculture and industry were slow to get going; there was a lack of manpower, while in many regions the occupying forces dismantled what machinery was left.

The Soviet occupation created a system of ration cards for the Soviet Occupation Zone, in effect on June 12, 1945. Allocated amounts were based on categories of consumers from I to V.

Category I: heavy industry workers and functionaries

Category II: light industry

Category III: workers

Category IV: office workers

Category V: other (children, pensioners, handicapped individuals, unemployed, and former members of the NSDAP)

In July, this allocation system was tightened further in that unemployed individuals as well as former members of the NSDAP were no longer receiving any ration cards.

The nickname for the ration cards given to children, pensioners, and handicapped individuals was the "cemetery card," since the allowed amount was hardly sufficient to sustain life. Meanwhile, many of the items on the cards, e.g., bread, meat, fat, sugar, potatoes, and other foods, were not regularly available. When they were, there would be a public announcement. When flour, rutabagas, or potatoes were to be had, people waited in line for hours. The portions became smaller, and more water would be added to an already watery flour soup.

In the western zones under the administration of the Allied Powers, the ration cards were more generous, and children received additional nutrition through school programs and the like. Still, there were frequent shortages. Christa's cousin Mareti, who lived in the American zone in Bavaria in the first years after the war, describes her brother's growing skills in finding things on the black market. Mareti regularly visited the garbage cans of houses where Americans lived, looking for edible food that was thrown out. She was thrilled when finding oranges. The Americans would press them out and toss them into the garbage. Mareti learned to scrape them out for remnants of the precious juice. She also went out of town onto the fields, gleaning whatever was left after the harvest.

The harvest in 1946 was further affected by a hot, dry summer and a lack of fertilizer. Moreover, there was not enough coal for industry uses much less for heating, and by the winter months of 1946, people suffered from severe malnutrition and the inescapable cold.

As the daughter of a well-known general, Christa was repeatedly invited to dinner by officers of the Soviet army. She accepted with trepidation but was determined to make the best of it. In preparation, she lined her coat pockets with wax paper. At these dinners, she was careful to pretend to sip the copious amounts of vodka that were offered, even resorting to pouring the contents into her coat collar. Meanwhile, she stuffed all the food she could grab into her pockets, arriving home in triumph with a squishy mess of desperately needed sustenance for her mother and herself.

"You smell like a still," her mother said when Christa arrived at home, looking slightly pregnant with her pockets filled with food.

Survival skills once acquired are hard to unlearn. Christa

claimed that the German habit, so pronounced in the first decades after World War II, of disregarding lines and pushing toward the front of the line originated in these days when people were desperate to get food for their families.

Many years later, when we went strawberry picking in Long Island, Christa was remarkably swift in consuming vast amounts of strawberries all the while filling her baskets.

"They don't weigh me," she said cheerfully when we headed to the checkout desk. At receptions in New York City, Christa always knew where the best food items were to be had, prodding me to check them out and laughing at my reluctance.

And yet, Christa described her life in the dark years at the end of World War II as "the best of times and the worst of times." People shared what they had, and the generosity and helpfulness of her friends and neighbors kept her going.

Christa's friend Maria related an incident where her hosts had gathered for a meal consisting of an allotment of herrings, one per person, when the doorbell rang. An unexpected guest was at the door. The daughters jumped up, gathered all the plates, pulled out another, and reapportioned the fish, cutting a little piece off from all the others until they could construct a whole one. The guest was greeted with delight, and he apparently never noticed the constructed nature of his fish.

Christa and her friends got together as often as they could, partying at the slightest occasion such as an allotment of carrots or food filched from a Soviet officers' dinner.

They even celebrated carnival, complete with costumes. Once, Christa used some material she had managed to obtain for dyeing her hair bronze. Overnight it turned green, and it took months to return to its natural blonde.

One of Christa's stories I wish I could forget. One of the rooms in the house where Christa lived with her mother was occupied by a German officer and his wife. The officer had been a friend of Christa's father, and Erika regularly dropped in on the couple to chat, smoking one of her many cigarettes. One day in 1945, the Soviets came to arrest this officer.

Christa happened to be at home when she heard banging doors and voices shouting commands. Christa stuck her head out and saw Soviet soldiers on the landing in front of the couple's door, gripping the officer by his arms and about to lead him away. His wife tried to hang on to his jacket and was screaming while her husband kept saying, "Mutti, calm down. Please, Mutti, please, keep calm."

The soldiers dragged him toward the stairs. His wife screamed louder, and the echo filled the entire stairwell.

At that point, Erika had had enough. She slapped the woman in the face and hissed, "Is this what you want him to hear as he walks out of this house?" The woman subsided, whimpering and sobbing as the soldiers with their prisoner in tow reached the front door. Her husband never returned home and died along with many others in a prisoner-of-war camp in the Soviet Union.

Those screams are etched into my memory as if I had heard them myself, amplified by my grandmother's silence about this as well as about her losses.

Christa and her mother didn't need to talk about the fact that if Bogislav had come home to Altenburg at the end of the war, he probably would have met the same fate.

This scene must have been especially painful for Christa since Egloff was then in a prisoner-of-war camp in Russia.

On April 30, 1945, Egloff was first interred in a camp in Deutsch Eylau in West Prussia, today Ilawa in Poland, and was transferred to Krasny-Bor, western Smolensk.

A few of his postcards made it to his mother and Christa. He talked about being content and in good health. He worked as a carpenter and had been designated as the head of the group of internees. He was allowed to write only once a month.

His last card to Christa, written on January 13, 1946, was cheerful and careful to give no additional cause for concern. "We are in solid housing, and we have electricity and good winter clothes. So far it has been mild. Do not worry about me. I am learning to read Russian. I agree with everything you will plan for our future. There will always be a new beginning. We will find it together, keeping our hearts and minds open." After that, there are no more cards or letters.

During the first year under Soviet occupation, house searches were a regular feature of life. Soviet soldiers appeared, looking for contraband as well as for suspected spies and members of the German army in hiding. The term contraband is used loosely, in that these searches were mostly a form of looting. The Soviet authorities officially prohibited such actions, but in practice did not do much about them.

One day, soldiers, roaming through the house, came across Erika's dressing table, arrayed with her brushes, face powder, and lipsticks. One of them sat on the little stool, stared at the mirror above the table, and tried out the lipstick. Another one grabbed a wristwatch that lay on top of a chest of drawers.

"You can't have that," Erika barked at him, in situations like this unfailingly cool, composed, and unafraid. "Give it back."

The young man was so surprised by her commanding voice and air of authority that he sheepishly handed her the wristwatch.

Once, Christa managed to deflect the soldiers when they appeared at the front door. Dressed in her Red Cross uniform, she stepped outside, pulling the door shut behind her. "Oh, I am so sorry, I forgot my key," she said, shrugging her shoulders helplessly. The soldiers grumbled and went away.

Christa immediately ran as quickly as she could to friends in the artist and actors community and asked them for their help. Christa's friends agreed to help her without hesitation, and shortly thereafter Christa watched them walk down the road carrying rugs, silverware, small pieces of furniture, and paintings. All of these things reappeared later when my grandmother was getting ready to leave for the west.

Members of this community were largely left alone by the Soviets and not harassed by house searches. They enjoyed a protected status. They were expected to play a role in the process of "cultural reeducation" by acting in certain plays, writing to disseminate propaganda, or producing artwork that fitted in with the desired ideological framework; therefore, the occupying Soviet authority did not want to alienate them.

The Soviets were not alone in this; other occupying forces also used the medium of culture in their efforts to reeducate Germans. This explains why art and cultural activities thrived in the immediate aftermath of the war even while much of the country was still in ruins. The organization Altenburger Werkstaetten is a good example of this. Altenburger Werkstaetten supported applied arts in and around Altenburg with the stated goal of participating in the rebuilding of everything that was lost in terms of art and culture in the preceding decades.

In the first months after the end of World War II, Christa worked as a Red Cross nurse. However, on November 15, 1945, she received a letter expressing regret that she could not be employed any further and thanking her for her service "assisting suffering residents."

From April 1, 1946 to January 15, 1947, Christa worked for Altenburger Werkstaetten C. Hoppe und K. Wolf. The certificate described her work as *Heimarbeit*, work done at home.

Altenburger Werkstaetten played a central role in the development of an exhibit at the Lindenau Museum in Altenburg in October 1946. It drew on local artists and craftsmen as well as those who had been displaced from their homes in other parts of Germany to prepare works in graphic design, drawing, woodwork, metalwork, textiles, and other applied arts and crafts.

While engaged in this work, Christa also started to look around for alternatives, increasingly worried that she was going to be forced to work in heavy industry.

On March 11, 1947, Christa received a certificate of completion, testifying that she had finished the course work in a training program for interpreters between October 1, 1946 and February 20, 1947 and that she had passed the required written and oral examinations. She applied for a position to teach English in high school, declaring herself qualified on the strength of her acquisition of English in school and her interpreter training program. She was accepted and assigned to a class of eighth-graders. The students laughed at her, amused by her married name Tippelskirch, which inspired funny pronunciations, and equally amused by her youth.

Meanwhile, Christa waited. She waited for Egloff to return home. She didn't want to leave Altenburg because she thought this was where Egloff would look for her when he returned. She waited to hear what had happened to her other family members and her friends. So, she continued trying to survive as best she could, and she waited.

People had begun to flee from East Prussia (today mostly part of Russian) in 1944, with whatever means possible— mostly this meant walking or traveling with horse-drawn carriages. Many of these treks went through Muttrin in the hopes of temporary respite before moving on to the West.

Among them were Zitzewitz relatives who had managed the stud farm Weedern in East Prussia, today a part of Russia. East Prussia was known for its horse breeding. The State Stud Trakehnen had been evacuated already in October 1944. However, private breeders like the Zitzewitz family in Weedern were not allowed to leave until January of 1945, when there was almost no time to escape. Tens of thousands of people and some 18,000 East Prussian horses began walking and driving westbound in the harsh winter of 1945. The Zitzewitz relatives were intent on trying to rescue some of their breeding stock of Trakehner horses. Several of their horses that stayed in Muttrin before continuing on their journey west became the basis of the new breeding stock in West Germany.

Many members of Egloff's family were displaced, fleeing from their homes as were many others.

Christa's family in Muttrin could not evacuate until March 6, 1945, two days before the Soviet Army reached Stolp since they had to await official permission from the government to do so. In the frantic attempt to get to one of the ships on the Baltic Sea, the group evacuating from Muttrin got split up, and some of them were forced back by the Soviet army. They were eventually expelled by the Polish government over the next few years.

Christa's cousin, Ingeborg von Zitzewitz, known as Pudel and born in 1925, had worked as a land girl during the war. In late February 1945, she went in search of her parents who lived in Stolp. There she got the news that they, along with about 1,000 other Stolp citizens, had committed suicide in the last weeks of the war. Surviving relatives, as well as historians, have speculated about the driving factors behind this action, one not restricted to Stolp but instead occurring in other localities throughout the region. Sheer mind-numbing exhaustion from years of war, fear of the invading army, loss of hope, shock over the growing realization of what their own country had done, and fear of reprisals may all have been a part of their decision. Pudel's mother sent her a letter; it expresses regret but does not offer much by way of explanation other than that they couldn't see a way out.

Upon receipt of this news, Pudel, at that time twenty years old, made her way west, traveling mostly on foot. She arrived at my grandmother's front door in Altenburg, dressed in a long man's shirt and little else. From there, she made it to

Munich where she worked as a secretary for Americans before moving to New York City. The subtext of her arduous journey across war-torn Germany was that she was repeatedly raped. I learned about this only through the veiled hints of other cousins, who spoke about that time with evident discomfort as if afraid to say more. In later years, Pudel started to write her memoirs; she never got beyond the early 1940s in her account, due to her failing health and death in 2011. When she talked to me about that time in her life, she never mentioned the brutalities to which she had been subjected; instead, she talked about how kind many people had been to her.

In 1947, while the border between what was to become the German Democratic Republic (GDR) and the Federal Republic of Germany (FRG) was still permeable, Christa escorted several children to the West, acting on behalf of friends who already had gone to the West or were trying to leave separately. For the crossing, she took a train to the edge of the Thüringer Wald and then walked across the demarcation line at night. I tried to picture Christa, muffled up, holding children by the hand, and walking along the Rennsteig, the famous hiking trail through the forest, in the dark.

Initially, the Allied Forces had sought to manage and control traffic between the zones but gradually relaxed restrictions in the Western zones. Approximately one and a half million Germans from a total of about seventeen million in East Germany had already left the Soviet occupation zone for the West between October 1945 and June 1946. According to estimates, more than three million left East Berlin, the Soviet occupation zone, and what was to become the German Democratic Republic (GDR) between 1945 and 1961. About one million of these had fled or been expelled from regions farther east at the end of World War II and its aftermath, landing in towns like Altenburg before trying to move on toward the West. Starting in the fall of 1946, restrictions were increasingly tightened between the zones in the west and Soviet zones. More border guards were deployed and unofficial crossings reinforced with ditches and barricades. Nevertheless, until 1952, the border remained somewhat permeable, and there was a fair amount of smuggling of goods in both directions.

While trying to survive in Altenburg, waiting to hear from Egloff, and figuring out what to do in the long run, Christa wrote letters. As one of the few people in her circle of friends and family with the same address, she passed on any news to others as they came in. The fact that she wrote often and at great length is evidenced by the responses she received, thanking her for her extensive descriptions and thoughtful comments. She wrote to Egloff's mother and his adoptive mother, both of whom were anxiously awaiting word from Egloff. These women reported at great length about their relatives, in particular, two war widows with six children between them who were making their way to the West. In later years, Christa continued to reach out to all the members of Egloff's extended family, and they were always a part of our lives.

At the same time, Christa received letters from other relatives who described leaving their homes in the East ahead of the approaching Soviet army.

With the same sense of responsibility for everyone with whom she ever had been in contact, Christa wrote regularly to Heinrich's mother. Heinrich's mother in turn responded with lengthy descriptions of her son's last days, thanking Christa for the happiness she gave him. She expressed her wishes for the well-being of Christa's husband. The bitter subtext of Heinrich's profound disappointment and heartache when Heinrich received the news from Christa breaking off their long-standing relationship is inescapable.

In one particularly painful letter to Christa, Heinrich's mother referred to her son's thoughts about this and his fear that the pressure from Christa's family would be too strong for her to resist. Heinrich told his mother, "It seems as if the constant negative feedback from [Christa's] mother combined with the fact that my letters are often delayed have drained her and worn down her resistance."

Heinrich's mother spoke of her gratitude for the fact that her son did not live to see the announcement of Christa's engagement to Egloff, posted a few days after Heinrich's death.

"Dear Christa, despite everything I still would like to call you by that name in recognition of the many happy hours you gave our son. ....His last letter reached us after his death.

He wrote on November 6, 1944, and he told us that you had dissolved the engagement. He was killed on December 9, 1944. I hope he didn't see the announcement of your engagement in the German news. Of course, I wish that decision had happened later and that my dear boy would not have had to suffer the most painful loss of his life. Initially, I couldn't help but worry whether perhaps that course of events let him be less careful in the field than he would have been otherwise."

After Christa's death, a friend of hers who had known about Heinrich claimed that he had essentially courted death on the battlefield.

The correspondence broke off when Christa left Altenburg for the last time in 1949.

In 1947, Christa began writing to the Red Cross, worried about not having heard from Egloff for a long time. The German Red Cross regretfully told her that it was very diffi- cult to determine exactly in which prisoner-of-war camp Egloff may have been. Increasingly desperate, she contacted a British friend of Egloff who lived in England and asked him for helping her with contacts to the British Red Cross. Robert

Neave promised Christa he would do his best. The British Red Cross responded repeatedly, with careful, polite phrases expressing regret about the difficulty of learning more about what had happened to individual soldiers.

Finally, in April 1948, a hastily written postcard from a soldier, returning from prison, reported that Lieutenant von Tippelskirch had died of typhus in February 1946.

"It's possible that there is a mistake since this soldier didn't know his first name, but in my heart I know it's true," Christa wrote to one of her closest friends. "I haven't had the courage yet to tell my mother-in-law; she already lost her other two sons and her husband."

Egloff's father had died in Tscherepowez, Russia, in November 1945, and his two brothers had already lost their lives in 1944. Egloff's mother, by then already in Gross-Weden in the north of Germany and living a refugee existence with her widowed nieces and their six children, all sleeping in the dining room of friends, wrote to Christa in December 1948 after receiving the news about Egloff.

She thanked Christa for letting her know. She asked after Christa's mother and wished her all the best for Christmas. As an aside, she described one of the almost daily scenes at train stations in the west, where relatives would stand on the platforms, hoping the next train would bring their sons or husbands. "It is so distressing to watch prisoners of war return from Russia as ruins of their former selves. I am almost grateful to know now that my son will never come home like that."

"Please don't say anything," Christa wrote to a close friend. "I have an indescribable horror of having to talk about it. I can't bear it; most of all I can't bear the expressions of sympathy. When no one knows about it, there is a certain protective barrier. I don't know what to say. I can't feel or think. Please don't write."

Christa learned more details about Egloff's last days only

several years later when another returning soldier wrote to Egloff's mother. He described Egloff's attempts to learn Russian and his struggles with pronunciation. The officers in camp took turns giving presentations about various subjects to their fellow inmates; perhaps Egloff talked about American criminal law, something he had studied while attending college in America. They worked from six in the morning until six or seven at night. Malnutrition and disease were draining everyone, and every day at least three or four of the prisoners died. When Egloff got sick, he was transferred to the hospital wing. His friend was able to visit him there. Egloff spoke to him through the open door, apparently in good spirits. He died during the night. In the morning, the prisoners watched from behind a wire fence as the bodies of those who died during the night were carried away for burial.

Now, there was no point in waiting any longer, and Christa began to plot her exit strategy. She decided to leave her mother in Altenburg for the time being until she could arrange for housing in the West. Robert Neave, Egloff's friend in England who had helped her with contacting the British Red Cross, offered to host her in his family's home. Christa obtained a travel permit from the Soviets, after convincing them that she wanted to improve her knowledge of English.

In 1949, Christa traveled to Berlin where she got a seat on an empty coal plane on its way back to the United Kingdom. For over a year, after the Soviets had blocked off transport and electricity to West Berlin, Allied planes dropped over two thousand million tons of food, medication, and coal to the beleaguered residents. Inspired by the candy dropped off by American cargo planes, West Berliners referred to these planes as *Rosinenbomber* or Raisin Bombers.

I was enthralled by Christa's description of sitting in the chilly and dirty airplane, nauseous, dizzy and overcome by the noise. The pilot invited her to sit in the cockpit when they reached the cliffs of Dover and began pointing out landmarks to her.

Christa arrived in England in the spring of 1949, with the dust from the coal plane permeating everything she owned, hungry, cold, and tired, having left behind a world in ruins, and facing an uncertain future.

Orsett House, an English manor house in Essex built by Samuel Bonham around 1740, was used as a school and a hospital during World War I. Subsequently, it was let out first to a Swedish aristocrat and then to Colonel Richard Neave. The owner, the Whitmore Trust, eventually sold the house in the 1980s, and it has now been subdivided into a series of apartments.

Orsett House, with its understated elegance and its well-kept formal gardens that seamlessly connected to gently flowing fields and a meandering brook, was a surreal and disorienting experience for Christa. Her hosts' way of life belonged in another time, bound by conventions, social class, and cultural expectations governing every single aspect of life, while seemingly largely unaffected by the years of war. In addition to Colonel Neave and his wife, several young people lived in the house. They spent much of their time lounging around in their tennis whites or going riding.

The family of Colonel Neave welcomed Christa as the widow of Egloff, a friend of their son Robert. Everybody was polite, but Christa could not shake the feeling of being an alien, moreover one from a country that had been at war with England.

She found the transition to a country at peace almost more than she could bear. She missed the sharp reality of life in wartimes and in an occupied zone after the war—there was a sense of certainty in living in constant fear—whether it was the bomb attacks in the last years of the war or the fears that came with living under Russian occupation, the daily worries about food, the lack of warm water for washing, the merciless cold. In the first months in England, there was nothing she could hold on to, stuck in her grief for all that was lost, unable to envision her future, and bewildered without the need for the self-discipline that years of war and its aftermath had imposed on her.

A peculiar problem was that Christa was always hungry. For years, she had been consuming large amounts of watery flour soup with bits of cabbage and rutabaga thrown in on good days. When confronted with delicate slices of thin ham and cucumber sandwiches—undoubtedly more nutritious— she was still desperately hungry. The kitchen staff began to befriend her, secretly augmenting her diet with porridge and other bulk food until her system adjusted.

In a letter to a friend after Christa arrived in Bonn in 1950, she wrote that she had felt constrained and tense while in England. In part, this was because she still shied away from thinking about all that had happened to her, afraid of losing control. At the same time, living a life of relative luxury did not shield her adequately from all the thoughts that came rushing in.

Christa, struggling with grief, disorientation, and a sense of living in limbo, was thrilled when she started receiving mail from friends in Germany. One friend regularly supplied her with reading materials while also sending care packages to Christa's mother in Altenburg. When friends visited, she would meet them in London, feeling that it was not her right to host them at Orsett House.

Meanwhile, by late 1949 Christa knew that the interlude in England had to come to an end. She worried about her mother alone in Altenburg and wanted to bring her to the West as soon as possible. A relative helped Christa to obtain the appropriate paperwork that allowed her to travel to West Germany and to establish residence there where it would be easier to start the process of getting her mother out of Altenburg.

Many years later, I accompanied my mother on a trip to England. She showed me many of her favorite places. She remembered them with fondness as if the sense of alienation, the feelings of constraint and confusion, and the grief mixed with fear of the future had been wiped from her mind. She was thrilled and excited to see a performance of *Richard III* at the theater. We went to Harrods to buy tea, traveled to the Cotswolds, and visited Oxford, splurging on tea with clotted cream and scones at the famous pub The Mitre, which figures in Dorothy Sayer's novel *Gaudy Night*.

Christa's gift for finding happiness never abandoned her even when she felt lost and lonely and without a roadmap for the future.

7

RED PHOENIX

"I don't rent to foreigners."

Christa blinked, momentarily at a loss for words. She had been walking around for days in search of an apartment in Bonn, Germany, and was tired and despondent after inspecting spaces that amounted to little more than broom closets. Finally, she had come upon a small one-bedroom that might work for her and her mother.

"But I am not a foreigner," Christa exclaimed.

"But you are not from here," the prospective landlady responded. After some pleading, she eventually relented.

This was Christa's introduction to Bonn in 1950.

The old center of the city was largely reduced to rubble, leaving only the lonely towers of the Bonn Minster, one of Germany's oldest churches, dating back to the 12th century. Photographs from that year show streetscapes bordered by fields of rubble and unattractive buildings hurriedly turned into temporary offices to accommodate the various branches of the young government.

I suspect that this sight did not disturb Christa's balance; she had seen worse in Berlin and other towns and cities in the East. The provincialism that she encountered was something else. Her experiences in those years left her with an attitude of disdain and reserve concerning the new Federal Republic of Germany, which she managed to shake only in the last decades of her life.

Bonn's defining and easily most dramatic feature is the Rhine with a stunning mountain range on the other shoreline across from the town. Its Baroque mansions, stately villas, and timber framework houses, the university with its imposing complex dating back to the 1800s, and pleasant parks surrounded by forests and agricultural land are in odd contrast with the seemingly interminable stretch of administrative buildings erected in the years after the war. Ironically, the young government initially found accommodations in abandoned military building complexes and barracks, an awkward legacy of the Third Reich.

Even though Frankfurt might have been the logical choice for the capital of the new Federal Republic of Germany, since it already had many of the required facilities, the politicians preferred Bonn because it sent the message that this was only a temporary solution, a stand-in for Berlin, which would eventually become the capital of a unified Germany.

The neighboring town Bad Godesberg, later incorporated into the larger city of Bonn, became the abode of government officials, foreign dignitaries, and diplomats. It also featured the remnants of a fortress with a tower on top of a hill overlooking the Rhine, dating back to at least the 13th century. As a child, I was blissfully unaware of the destruction that World War II had wreaked even in Bonn for all that compared to other towns and cities in Germany the damage was hardly as catastrophic. I was stunned when I came across a photograph of children playing on the debris of a Halifax bomber that had exploded in the Kottenforst on March 27, 1943. I had spent a lot of time playing in that same forest since it was within walking distance from our house.

Over twelve million refugees and exiles from eastern parts

of Germany, in particular, East Prussia, Silesia, and Pomerania, and eastern territories formerly occupied by the Nazi regime had fled to the Allied occupation zones of Germany and Berlin after the end of the Second World War. This included over one million from Pomerania alone in search of a new home.

In 1950, the country was still struggling with absorbing the vast number of refugees, while at the same time trying to rebuild its devastated cities. More than half of residential space had been destroyed during the war. To address the most pressing need, local and federal authorities focused on the construction of housing. Anyone familiar with German postwar construction can easily recognize the buildings built in the first decade after the war, constructed as quickly as possible, with cheap materials, a minimalist approach to design, and exposed concrete.

It is hard to overestimate the tremendous pressure felt by residents in the west when confronted with an influx of people as had never happened before. Moreover, in the aftermath of World War II, Germany had to absorb not only millions of refugees from formerly German lands; there also were millions of ethnic Germans arriving in the West. They had been expelled from Eastern European countries, often after having been forced to work in labor camps under atrocious conditions. Many of these ethnic Germans did not speak German, and this contributed to their being viewed with suspicion and resentment by the local population, themselves already struggling to get by, faced with a lack of housing and paying jobs.

Christa's relatives and many of her friends were among the refugees from Pomerania, East Prussia, and Silesia. Shortly after arriving in Germany, Christa visited her deceased husband's family in Lower Saxony. As two war widows, with six children between them, as well as a mother and an aunt to take care of, they struggled to rebuild their lives. They found refuge in a makeshift barn on a piece of land in Bordenau, Lower Saxony. With remarkable foresight, a relative had deeded this plot to Egloff's cousins before the end of the war. One sister, with help from the children, grew vegetables. The other worked as a physical therapist in town and also transported the vegetables to the local market on a motorcycle.

Cramped for space and short of the bare necessities for life, they welcomed Christa with open arms. The generosity of spirit that people exhibited in the years after the war inspired both Christa and her mother in later years to help and to give back wherever they could. All of these relatives lived with us at various points in their lives, such as when one of them was between jobs or attending a school or a university nearby. The oldest had a room in my parents' house on Long Island and spent many summers with us.

Christa found a job as a secretary in the protocol office of the German Foreign Service (*Auswärtiges Amt*) in Bonn.

The first year in Bonn, Christa spent mostly alone. In a letter to a friend, she mentions several stints in a hospital without going into any details. I suspect it may have been a form of hepatitis since she was repeatedly affected by jaundice and hepatitis in later years. She talked about hiding out at work to avoid having to talk to people. Adjusting to her new life was a challenge, and it was nearly impossible to avoid thinking about everything that had happened to her over the last years. With remarkable insight, she mentioned her tendency to ignore those things she could not control and to refrain from talking about things that were troubling her. If one didn't talk about something, it was easier to pretend it never existed. In another letter, she described her sense of utter isolation during her months in England, trapped in a surreal existence and unable to shake off a sense of bitterness.

However, gradually the hard shell she had developed around herself began to crack. Having an income helped, and more importantly, she began to meet people and make friends.

Meanwhile, her mother Erika was still in Altenburg. By 1950, it had become increasingly challenging to leave the newly formed German Democratic Republic (GDR), also referred to as East Germany, and consisting of the regions that had been under Soviet occupation. Eventually, people were permitted to leave with nothing but what they were wearing if they were permitted to leave at all. Even before the formal constitution of the GDR in 1949, the removal of property by people relocating to the West was becoming increasingly difficult.

Erika was determined to send as much of her property to the West as possible.

As soon as Christa had signed the lease on her apartment in Bonn, she told her mother to begin packing up and to prepare for her departure.

Erika began by sending small items in the mail, a few pieces of silverware, small icons, and porcelain, careful to keep the packages under the legal limit of fourteen pounds.

Christa was cheered by the piecemeal arrival of treasured bits and pieces from the past.

Meanwhile, Erika's regular visits to the post office began to attract the attention of the *Kriminalpolizei*, the criminal investigation department of the GDR. Occasionally postal clerks, who had come to know her well, would wave her away when there was a chance of her being watched, telling her to come back on another day when it was safe. Erika kept track of all these people, and in later years, she regularly sent care packages to everyone who had helped her.

One item had already traveled to the west, the painting by Franz Gerhard von Kügelgen, the *Madonna of the Veil*, which belonged to my grandmother. Helga, one of Christa's closest friends, coincidentally a descendant of the painter, who was already living in the west, traveled to Altenburg to visit Erika, and offered to take the painting back with her. Together, they carefully removed the wooden frame and detached the painting from its backing. Helga rolled it up and hid it under her coat. She managed to reach Berlin, where she left the painting with friends. Years later, a relative retrieved it from there.

In the summer of 1951, Erika convinced a Soviet commissar to allow her the use of an open cattle transport wagon for her move. With the help of friends, she loaded the wagon with her remaining possessions and began the eight-hour train journey to Bonn, where she arrived in mid-August 1951.

Christa had given some thought about what to do once her mother would arrive with her rescued furniture. She approached the Dutch ambassador to Germany at that time and presented the surprised gentleman with an unusual proposal. The ambassador happened to be in dire need of appropriate pieces for his ambassadorial residence. Christa suggested that he could use all her furniture for the time being, provided that he restored it. Remarkably, the ambassador agreed to this deal. As soon as Christa was able to arrange for a larger apartment for her mother, she retrieved the furniture. Some of it is now in my home in America.

In a letter to a friend, Christa described Erika as "small and thin," overwhelmed by all that had happened to her and struggling to adjust to the new world in which she found herself. Erika was just fifty at the time.

"She has become so small and thin, so helpless. I always feel I could pick her up and stick her in my pocket. Now, she is no longer called upon to demonstrate courage, strategic thinking, or discretion, and with the lack of such demands, her strength continues to shrink. She is always in tears when I come home. Her nerves are shot—an inevitable reaction to the war years, six years of living in the East Zone, and countless moments of danger. I always remember how it was for me when I first arrived in England. I couldn't bear the feeling of not having to worry, the experience of sitting down at a table laid with food, and the certainty of a warm bath. I literally craved danger, fear, and deprivation. It will be similar for my mother. I have to find tasks for her and confront her with problems so that she continues to believe she has an important role to play."

Christa also talked about the changes to the personality exhibited by people who lived in the East Zone for any length of time. "Her thoughts have become strange to me. I must rediscover my own mother."

As an aside, it is appropriate to comment on the use of the term East Zone.

Before the formation of the German Democratic Republic in 1949, its entire territory was called the East Zone, which meant the zone under Soviet occupation as opposed to the zones in the west under French, British, and American occupation. However, the name East Zone continued to be used for many years as a synonym for the GDR; its usage often implied pejorative connotations.

Erika was fiercely loyal and generous to a fault, always willing to help others. As soon as she was settled in Bonn, she began the first of what were to be annual initiatives to show her gratitude to all who had helped her during World War II and its aftermath. This took on the form of an annual *Bahnhofsmission* which she operated out of her apartment. This Bahnhofsmission (train station mission) was a charity originally organized in 1897 by Protestant and Catholic churches, to provide help to those in need, and it operated in every large railway station throughout Germany. Using her income from her widow's pension, Erika purchased vast amounts of coffee, tea, sugar, cocoa, sweets, shower gel, soap, baking ingredients, clothing, and bed linen, among other items. It took weeks to pack everything and take it to the post office. The little hallway and the guestroom in her apartment were staging areas for this endeavor.

Of course, my grandmother was hardly the only one engaged in this activity. Many West Germans regularly sent packages to East German relatives—the famous *Westpakete*, wrapped in brown paper and tied with string. Each package had to be marked as a present and could not contain anything considered trade goods. Sending money was strictly prohibited, even though senders tried to circumvent this by sticking bills into chocolate bar wrappings or coffee cans. Some packages featured a hollow or double bottom where senders hid things that were not allowed, especially magazines and money. Magazines, even when out of date, offered entertainment and colorful glimpses into the world beyond the border. Money, that is, D-Mark, was especially welcome since it could be used for purchases of luxury goods only sold in so-called *Intershops* where products from the West were sold.

Ironically, the East German government, while initially hostile to this activity and seeking to hinder it at every turn by instituting regulation after regulation, eventually included the regular west packages, in particular, the steady supply of coffee, among other items, as part of their budget planning, since it reduced the need for expensive imports.

When Erika started a new life in Bonn, she was still youthful in appearance and strikingly beautiful. As the widow of a high-ranking officer, Erika received a pension and was able to live comfortably. Several men, whom she met after the war, admired her. One proposed to her repeatedly. However, my grandmother wouldn't have it. She was not willing to budge from the routines that she had carved out for herself.

"Why does your mother have to do her laundry on the one day I can come and visit her?" one man asked Christa. He eventually gave up and disappeared.

That story always made me sad. After arriving in Bonn in 1951, my grandmother proceeded to close one door after another, choosing to live within narrowly defined parameters while maintaining a stolid silence about the past.

She had internalized many of the restrictions from her life under Soviet occupation and translated these into her existence in Bonn, often stating categorically, "But you can't do that."

"You are not supposed to do that."

"That's not allowed."

"The neighbors will complain."

"You can't do that." I feared and hated that phrase even as a child while still in Germany. After I had lived in America for a while, I had an almost visceral reaction to this type of ingrained acceptance of restrictions on behavior. I must admit that nothing pleased me more than the blatant disregard of any of these rules by the jovial trash removers who helped us clear out my grandmother's apartment in Bonn after her death. They took a long thoughtful look at her balcony on the sixth floor, overlooking a small front yard next to the pedestrian sidewalk, and then, without further ado, began to toss the old mattresses out onto the sidewalk, where they collected them and loaded them onto their truck. Christa looked at me, grinning all over her face.

My grandmother adhered to her chosen schedule as if any form of deviation spelled disaster; her life permanently dwindled to a desperate clinging to rules and regulations. Meanwhile, hidden underneath that nearly impermeable layer of rigidity and inflexibility was a volcanic temperament, the eruptions of which were painful and unforgettable for all of us.

In contrast, Christa was almost like a shapeshifter, able to adjust to new circumstances and even to embrace them with remarkable flexibility and resilience. As she recovered from the experiences during and after the war, her unquenchable thirst for life and her customary habit of making plans for the future reasserted itself.

Walking past a small shop with fine porcelain and glass-
ware and glancing at the window display, she saw a set of
dinnerware made by Villeroy & Boch, a German manufacturer of ceramics, in a pattern called Red Phoenix. Each plate
was festooned with colorful birds with sweeping tails, perched
on flowering trees. The dominant color was a warm red. After
blinking at the price, she marched inside the store and bought
one plate. As soon as she could afford it, she bought another,
and then another.

This became the dinnerware we used all the years of my
childhood. I still have a nearly complete set.

✤ 8 ✤

WOLF ULRICH

"Oh, that's what you look like."

Spoken in a tone of shock, these words were the first Wolf Ulrich von Hassell said when he met Christa in 1951.

In reflection of the relatively small social circle to which both Christa and Wolf Ulrich belonged, their worlds had overlapped repeatedly in the 1940s even though they had never encountered each other. Wolf Ulrich had heard about Christa from friends.

Christa had met her first husband Egloff in the family home of a friend whom Wolf Ulrich was interested in. By a bizarre coincidence, Egloff had also been attracted to this same woman. She later became my godmother.

After Christa arrived in Bonn, one of her closest friends introduced her to several people. "And this is how it has come about that I meet and spend time with people whom one might well describe as 'the daughters and sons of the fathers,' she wrote in a letter.

"That is, they are all individuals who grew in relatively glamorous circumstances, often abroad, as children of ambassadors and envoys, thereby imbibing a familiarity and knowledge of the world of the past, which lends them a unique charm, and yet also prevents them from detaching themselves from the strong impressions of the past and to move beyond an existence of the sons and daughters of important personages to become individuals in their own right."

The reference to "sons and daughters" included those whose parents had in one form or

another been involved in the resistance against Hitler, frequently paying for this with their lives, as well as those who, like Christa, were seeking to rebuild their lives after their families had lost everything during the war.

For Christa, it was a relief to meet people who understood her feelings of loss and grief, adrift in a new world and without a home. Many of them had experienced a similar kind of uprooting and like her struggled with a troubled uncertainty about how to meet the future. They shared many of her values and the painful awareness that the country of their childhood was gone, leaving behind rubble and a moral-ethical framework in tatters. This half-familiar world became a source of comfort and also helped to open new doors. On the other hand, with a fascinating astuteness, she also noted the following.

"These are mostly extremely intelligent and capable individuals; however, I often wonder how their lives would turn out if they didn't have all these traditions. I believe they might succeed in the world much more rapidly. Now, they expend a great deal of energy on ensuring that the spirits of the past—and it is a lost world—not be allowed to dwindle into silence."

Reading this moved me to tears. I saw my father in front of me, complex, sensitive, and bearing all the burdens of the past. It just had never dawned on me how clearly Christa had understood this when she first met him. Like others whom Christa befriended in Bonn, my father for all the years that I knew him struggled to bridge the gap between several worlds. Having spent much of his childhood and youth abroad, the Germany he carried with him in his heart was based on a world of culture and a set of clearly delineated standards of values and moral-ethical parameters of behavior. All this was ripped apart by the Nazis, culminating in the execution of his father in 1944.

As I grew up, I became increasingly aware of the emotional fragments with which my father had to contend as someone who survived while so many of his peers had died during World War II while at the same time trying to overcome his sense of alienation and lack of connection to modern-day Germany.

Wolf Ulrich von Hassell was born in Genoa, Italy in 1913, where his father Ulrich von Hassell served as consul general, and spent part of his childhood in Rome, Barcelona, and Copenhagen. He studied law at the Universities of Tübingen and Königsberg, East Prussia, before receiving his doctorate in jurisprudence from the University of Würzburg. Shortly before the start of World War II, he joined the navy. However, early in 1939, he fell ill, stricken down by a rare lung disease. He spent the next three years in a sanatorium in Switzerland.

Wolf Ulrich never fully recovered from this disease, subject to debilitating bouts of bronchitis and as well as attacks of asthma for the rest of his life. His health was not improved by the effects of an upbringing that frowned at any efforts to take care of oneself as self-indulgent mollycoddling. In my grandmother Hassell's philosophy, best described as a form of Prussian asceticism gone rogue, being ill, hungry, or tired were signs of weakness. Wolf Ulrich had internalized these maxims and ignored discomfort of any kind to the point that it often became detrimental. He repeatedly landed in the hospital with a raging infection or severe pneumonia because of his habit of disregarding any health issues that came up.

While Wolf Ulrich was in the sanatorium in Arosa, Switzerland from 1939 until 1942, his father Ulrich von Hassell, a prominent member of the resistance movement against Hitler, visited him regularly. Ulrich von Hassell made use of this opportunity to meet with representatives of foreign governments in the hopes of thereby conveying the goals of the German resistance to foreign governments and obtaining their support. This engagement on behalf of the resistance movement deepened the friendship between father and son, and throughout the next years, Wolf Ulrich was privy to all of his father's activities.

Still greatly weakened from his illness, from 1942 on, Wolf Ulrich worked for the Fachgruppe Pharmazeutische Industrie in Berlin as an attorney. To me the fact that he worked for this organization, which published information about pharmaceuticals, is funny—all the years that I knew my father, he hated and despised medicine and resisted taking pills as much as he could. Throughout those same years, he was in constant contact with his father who discussed the opposition's plans with him. After the July 20th assassination attempt in 1944, Wolf Ulrich managed to place a call to his father, warning him of the failure of the attempt. Rather than trying to flee, his father chose to wait for the Gestapo and was arrested in his office shortly thereafter. Many involved in the attempt were arrested almost immediately. Others tried to get away and were hunted down; some of my father's close friends went underground until the end of World War II. Wolf Ulrich was the only member of his immediate family who was not arrested in the subsequent purge, an instance of the perverse illogical actions on the part of individuals representing the regime.

My father argued that many actions of the Gestapo were driven by fear, afraid of being accused of not having done enough or having done too much. After the failed attempt on July 20th, they were eager to sweep up anyone associated with the resistance movement. The Nazis argued that family members shared in the responsibility for a crime committed by one of its members and used this to justify the punishment of kin of people involved in the resistance. The term for this was *Sippenhaft*.

Consequently, after my grandfather's arrest, the Gestapo in Munich arrested my grandmother and my aunt. Wolf Ulrich, instead of going into hiding, immediately traveled to Munich. He went to the local Gestapo and berated them to the point where they were so astounded by his apparent conviction that he was inviolable that they became afraid of having overreached and released my grandmother and my aunt. Subsequently, Wolf Ulrich repeatedly visited the prison where his father was being held, again confounding the Gestapo by his lack of fear and his insistence on trying to see his father. He was not successful but managed to send his father cigarettes and paper for writing.

Meanwhile, Wolf Ulrich's younger sister, Fey, who lived in Italy, was arrested and separated from her two young sons. She spent the remaining months until the end of the war in a series of concentration camps for political prisoners and relatives of people involved in the resistance against Hitler. Fey wrote about her experiences in some detail in her book *Hostage of the Third Reich*.

Ulrich von Hassell was arrested on July 28, 1944 and executed on September 8, 1944.

Wolf Ulrich lived in an apartment in Potsdam until April 1945. After his father's execution, he spent his time trying to survive on an increasingly sparse diet while experiencing the feeling of being an outcast—friends of his crossed to the other side of the road when they encountered him out of fear of being associated with a member of the resistance. In anticipation of things to come and realistic about the possible nature of the much-hoped-for peace, he had found an old expatriate Russian lady to teach him Russian. In his free time, he rode his rickety bike through Berlin, increasingly battered and strewn with rubble, and repeatedly visited the prison at Prinz-Albrecht Strasse in Berlin where my grandfather had been kept before the trial in the hopes of retrieving his father's personal effects. Wolf Ulrich knew that his father had written extensively in the weeks prior to his execution because he mentioned this in his final letter to his wife. Just before the Soviets entered Berlin, my father finally convinced a Gestapo guard to help him. In the perverse orderliness displayed by the Gestapo and other representatives of the Third Reich, my grandfather's watch, his cigarette case, his signet ring, and his memoirs had been kept in a storage area in the basement of the building, and my father had to sign a piece of paper indicating that he had taken possession of these items. These were eventually published in 1994 under the title *Der Kreis schließt sich - Aufzeichnungen aus der Haft 1944.*

The last documentary prepared by Hitler's propaganda machine was entitled "Traitors before the People's Court," and focused on the trials of people accused in the 20th of July plot against Hitler. This documentary did not end up on the weekly newsreel that movie visitors were forced to endure during the years of World War II, perhaps in part because its producers realized that it might have the opposite effect from the one intended. The people who in Freisler's words were deemed "despicable swine" appeared at their trials in tattered clothing, deprived of all outer forms of dignity such as ties or jackets, and often showed visible signs of maltreatment during their incarceration; this actually served to emphasize the dignity and composure of these individuals. Afraid for themselves and their family members, shaken, and exhausted, they nonetheless remained steadfast in their convictions, even while aware of the probable outcome of what was nothing more than a kangaroo court presided over by a screaming and spitting Judge Freisler.

After the war, my father, along with other family members of individuals killed by Hitler, was invited, if one could use such a term, to view this documentary including the films Hitler had made of the executions. The knowledge that my father sat through this always fills me with horror. I suppose he felt it was a form of bearing witness and of keeping his father company after the fact. He never talked about it.

In the first year after the war, Wolf Ulrich devoted much of his energy to editing his father's wartime diaries and finding a publisher. He was consumed by the need to convey to the world the struggle of "another Germany" that had existed under the shadow of Hitler's regime. Several publishers in Germany turned down the project; in part, this was due to a lingering hesitation of touching any material bearing on Nazi history, in particular, written by someone whom a fair number of Germans considered a traitor. Eventually, Atlantis Verlag in Switzerland agreed to take on the project and published the diaries in 1946 under the title *Vom anderen Deutschland. Aus den nachgelassenen Tagebüchern 1938-1944.*

Wolf Ulrich participated in the process of rebuilding postwar Germany, an undertaking defined and limited by the remnants of the Nazi era as much as by the country's earlier history. In 1945-46, he advised the Americans on matters relating to the complicated process of denazification at all levels of society, economy, media, the judiciary, and politics. He was able to do so since the Americans had decided that given his father's history, Wolf Ulrich could be trusted. The Americans ultimately abandoned this undertaking in 1946, handing it over to the emerging West German government. In Germany, the process remained unpopular, and many Nazis maintained positions of power.

In 1951, Wolf Ulrich worked for one of the ministries in the young republic, the Federal Ministry for Food and Agriculture, where he was engaged in "setting prices of eggs," as Christa put it with amusement. He had also entered the Foreign Service training program to become a diplomat.

It is relatively easy to picture my father at that time when Christa first met him in 1951, almost forty, skinny, even starved looking, in part because of his illness, and in part because of an ingrained frugality that meant his kitchen cabinets were mostly bare of food. He was very proud of having cocoa that he could offer to Christa. While he enjoyed food, the concept of buying any for his own consumption eluded him.

Years later, when my mother and I joined my father in a hotel in New York City, where we lived for several months until we could find an apartment, it turned out that he had been living off a bizarre combination of milk and orange juice. He was quite proud of this culinary invention. In later years, he learned to make tea for my mother. It was an enormous production for him, but he did it faithfully and laboriously, spreading crumbs all over the kitchen as he cut toast, smeared butter and jam on small slices, and boiled the tea water to the point that it almost evaporated.

Christa, then 27 years old, was immediately attracted to Wolf Ulrich. She was bewitched by his sense of humor, his honesty, his entirely unself-conscious lack of interest in what other people thought of him, a characteristic that made him not only unimpeachable but also genuinely free and independent in his thoughts and opinions, and his ability to discuss any given topic with intelligence and a balanced perspective.

In a letter to a friend, with remarkable self-reflexive honesty, she mentioned her tendency to search for something familiar to her, describing herself as essentially conventional.

Meanwhile, Wolf Ulrich was anything but conventional; however, the world within which he operated was one that Christa understood and shared. They both moved with ease in various social circles and were fluent in several languages.

While Christa's family had been firmly rooted among the land-owning nobility in Pomerania, and Wolf Ulrich's family background placed him as a descendant of a line of military officers without any property to speak of other than that lost or gambled away by one ancestor, they shared a similarly peripatetic childhood, with many years spent abroad as a result of their respective fathers' employments.

Soon after their first meeting, Christa realized that she wanted to be with Wolf Ulrich. She was not greatly perturbed by the existence of several women with whom he was close. Quite the contrary, she befriended them. One of them coincidentally had been close to Christa's first husband as well.

However, Wolf Ulrich, whom Christa started to refer to as WU in her letters, was of a different caliber than Egloff or perhaps even Heinrich. He hesitated to make a commitment. He was too old, he told Christa, and too sick. Most likely he would die soon. He was too old to have children.

Christa had no such hesitations. She was determined to create a life for herself, and she knew she could do that with WU.

"No, you won't die," she told him firmly. "And you are not too old to have a family."

Eventually, he gave in.

This image of my father as reluctant to enter into a commitment is entirely believable to me. WU was unwavering in his sense of moral-ethical values, unshakeable in his convictions, unafraid of risk to himself for standing up for his beliefs, and steadfast and untiring in his defense of his children and anyone dear to him. However, when it came to acting on his own behalf, he preferred to withdraw, his ingrained skepticism exacerbated by his illness and his personal history that had left an indelible mark on him. Like many who had lived through the Nazi era and World War II, especially those associated with members of the resistance against Hitler, a portion of his inner makeup was forever fragmented. He had lost not only a family member and many friends but also was robbed of confidence in the future—having seen that there were no limits to the horrors a country can perpetrate.

For Christa, WU's steadfastness, honesty, and decency, combined with his cautious, even conservative approach to how to conduct his life, served as guardrails or counterweights for her willingness to take risks and to push forward. As annoying as his reluctance to make a quick decision could be, it was also served as a protective bulwark. It forced Christa to slow down when she was too apt to leap into action.

Of course, every marriage has its pitfalls. Christa in marrying WU had to contend with a formidable mother-in-law and the other Hassell family members.

Ilse von Hassell made much of her status as the widow of a man who sacrificed his life for what he believed in. In her opinion, a second marriage was tantamount to a betrayal. She was relentless in her adulation of her husband and made no effort to disguise her firm belief that no one else could measure up to him and that his actions accorded the family as a whole a special exalted status in the world.

My father reminded us that my grandmother's enormous sense of superiority regarding the Hassell family should not inspire us to get carried away by a similar sentiment—after all, the family is and was a family like any other with its fair share of individuals who gambled away family fortunes, drank themselves to death, were sent away for their misdeeds, or lived quiet, unremarkable if blameless lives. My great-grandfather who penned the first version of the so-called Family History made a similar point in his introduction.

"Writing the history of a family whose members never had any outstanding impact on the history and formation of their fatherland as statesmen, commanders of armies, or poets may perhaps be deemed an ungrateful sort of task; however, I take it upon myself anyway, because I believe one can learn a lot from the lives of one's ancestors, both those who are good models and those who are bad ones."

"Of course, I would never have married again," Ilse von Hassell told Christa witheringly in a snide reference to Christa's status as a war widow. She was also openly disdainful of Christa's occupation and sniffed at the thought of her oldest son marrying someone whom she deemed as a mere secretary. Moreover, she considered Christa to be a *Landpomeranze*, a pejorative term applied to girls from the countryside, mere country bumpkins with no manners or learning, and thought of Christa's family as barely noteworthy compared to the Hassell clan.

Fortunately, Christa had enough of a sense of humor and a well-developed sense of self to withstand this form of an emotional onslaught. When shaken and battered by my grandmother's dismissive arrogance, she reminded herself that while WU's family could only trace its ancestry back to the late 1600s with any real certainty, Christa's family on both her father's and her mother's side could trace back its history to the 1300s. To her credit, she was able to laugh at herself for treasuring such an ultimately entirely irrelevant historical detail. In later years, my parents liked to tease each other over this. "For you, history stops at the Thirty Years War," Christa would tell WU triumphantly.

On the day of the wedding, March 29, 1952, at my Hassell grandmother's house in Ebenhausen near Munich, Christa was afflicted with a head cold and the vestiges of another bout with jaundice. WU's older sister Almuth was a stunningly beautiful woman, who was very aware of this fact and not shy about rubbing it in. When Christa struggled with the bridal veil, Almuth took it from her. Flinging it over her shiny dark hair, she preened herself in the mirror. "Everything becomes me, of course," she said with a shrug and handed the veil back to Christa.

WU's younger brother, in charge of arrangements for the wedding dinner, squirreled away the good wine that a friend had presented for the occasion, with the argument that it would have been wasted in all the confusion of a wedding and was much better saved for another day.

All of these stories were hilarious for us when we grew up, but the darker side of the coin was the effect of a dysfunctional family on the younger members. My cousins had to bear the brunt of my Hassell grandmother's notions of child-rearing—which included, among other things, locking frightened youngsters into dark cabinets. My older brother also was exposed to this during a stay with my grandmother for several months. My younger brother, Adrian, and I did not spend as much time in her house without my parents, and hence, we escaped largely unscathed.

In my grandmother's eyes, her son had committed the unforgivable sin of becoming a diplomat. For her, that amounted to sacrilege and an attack on the memory of her husband, the only "true" diplomat in the family.

Christa was determined to make sure WU would be able to make a life for himself away from this emotional black hole of living as a satellite in the orbit of my Hassell grandmother.

Sadly, my father's brother and older sister never managed to detach themselves—unlike my father's younger sister Fey whose life in Italy had freed her to some extent. My father's older sister lived in a wing of my grandmother's house for the rest of her life, and my father's brother eventually built a house on a portioned-off section of her garden. It sat on a slope below the house, and every afternoon he would walk up the hill to join my grandmother for tea, often leaving his wife behind.

Before their church wedding, the young couple went to the civil registrar. The officiating individual, speaking with a full-throated Bavarian accent, spoke the momentous words pronouncing Christa and Wolf Ulrich to be married and then added, "Three DM, please." Three DM (D-Mark or Deutsche Mark) were roughly equivalent to ten dollars.

Christa and WU started to giggle. Baffled, the groom groped in his pockets and nudged his bride to see if she had any money with her. Fortunately, one of the witnesses could help out, lending them the requisite amount for the fee.

In a letter to a friend, reporting about her marriage to WU, Christa wrote, "I have arrived in a harbor."

9

MARRIED LIFE

"FROM A YOUNG HUSBAND," THE INSCRIPTION READS ON THE flyleaf of a small blue linen-bound volume by Honoré de Balzac, *A Bachelor's Establishment* containing Balzac's hilarious description of a bachelor existence.

This gift from WU to Christa was dated September 10, 1952. It was the first of a total of thirty-two volumes. Until 1971, Christa and WU continued to present each other with one or another volume of the collected works of Balzac, most of them with a personal inscription, often with an ironic reference to a particular phrase from Balzac or as straightforward expressions of love. At Christmas 1952, Christa wrote "to my 'bad husband,'" on the flyleaf of the little novella entitled *Harmony in a Marriage*, in mocking reference to the fact that marriages often are anything but harmonious. In 1954, Christa chose Balzac's *Droll Stories* and pasted a copy of a woodcut into the book. Underneath the image of a couple reposing awkwardly side by side in a narrow wooden bed, she penned an inscription, "Song without words."

My favorite inscription appears in a volume entitled *Lost Illusions*: "To my darling WU, as a consolation for all the illusions lost in two years of marriage. March 29, 1954."

This collection is a perfect recapitulation of their marriage, founded on a willingness to take a long-term view of things, always with plans that extended far into the future, a shared wealth of literature and poetry as well as a system of values, and most of all, a sense of humor.

Christa liked to relate an incident a few years into their marriage. WU was domestically challenged to put it mildly. He knew how to boil water and at some point in his life had learned how to fry an egg, but that was the extent of his culinary skills. This was compounded by a tendency to get frustrated with himself. Such frustration was never once directed against us; it was more of a desperate railing against himself and his helplessness or incompetence in certain situations. The setting for this particular encounter was the kitchen; Christa and WU were unpacking. Something went wrong, and WU got upset. He picked up a plate from a tall stack and smashed it. Calmly, Christa handed him another one. By the time the third plate ended on the floor, they were both laughing.

In 1952, in the first year of their marriage, Christa and WU devised a roadmap for their future. Christa always had a plan and always thought in terms of the long-term. She acted quickly and without hesitation when a good deal came her way, often after having persuaded my cautious and skeptical father to go along with her plans. One of their first acts was to open an account at the newly formed Bausparkasse, a savings and loan institution set up in Germany after WWII. The Bausparkasse was supposed to restore a depleted housing market, help families accumulate capital, and assure a more equitable distribution of assets in the Federal Republic of Germany. This made it possible for my parents to build a little plot of land on the outskirts of Bonn, where they later built a house.

When I was a child, money was never a topic of discussion at the dinner table. It was considered in bad taste to mention it. My parents were frugal, yet also made many things available to us such as ballet, judo, violin, and flute lessons to name a few, and, most importantly from our point of view, riding lessons. How they managed this on my father's initially sparse government salary remains a mystery to me to this day. Meanwhile, even though money was not a permitted topic of discussion, we all knew the term *Bausparkasse*.

Christa and WU lived in Bonn from 1952 until 1954. WU had completed his training period and started his career at the German Foreign Service.

Their happiness was only marred by WU's continued frail health and frequent severe cases of bronchitis and Christa's near-death experience when she went into labor at the birth of their eldest child, my brother Agostino, in 1953. Sadly, this turned out to be a recurring pattern at the birth of her two other children. After her third disastrous delivery, a doctor told her that she should not risk any further pregnancies.

In 1954, WU was posted to Rome where he served as a junior officer, a so-called legation counsellor (Legationsrat), at the German Embassy. It was to remain WU's only bilateral assignment. In all subsequent posts, he worked at the multilateral level.

As a curious parallel, my grandfather had been posted to Rome immediately after World War I, where he considered one of his principal tasks to ensure that Italians would once again come to see Germans with a modicum of respect, in his words as "housebroken." For WU, Rome was like coming home. He was completely fluent in Italian, and his younger sister Fey lived in Rome.

Christa embraced her life as the wife of a diplomat whole-heartedly and without ever giving us the feeling that she was missing something by not returning to graduate school or working in her field of art and art history. Meanwhile, the initial adjustment in Italy was a challenge for her. WU laughed as he watched Christa struggle with the habitual chaos and unpredictability of life, whether it was a strike, a bewildering forest of Byzantine regulations, or a disruption of water or electricity supplies. He told her that she needed to relax and learn to *arrangiare*, that is, to make do and go with the flow.

Christa listened and learned quickly. She became fluent in Italian, adding it to her ability to speak French and English. She was thrilled by the rich fabric of culture all around her and by the easygoing atmosphere, a stark contrast to dour Germany in the postwar years. She also reveled in the presence of friends from earlier times, with whom she reconnected, including a friend from her university days in Prague who now lived in Florence, as well as her sister-in-law Fey. As a testament to the degree to which both Christa and WU loved living in Rome, they thought they might retire in Italy and held on to this idea for many years.

My brother Adrian was born in 1956, and I followed in 1957.

In 1959, WU was posted to Brussels where he represented the Federal Republic of Germany at the Common Market, later known as the European Union. It was the first of WU's multilateral assignments. The Common Market had just been in existence for two years, and its members were grappling with the complex problems of how to remove trade barriers between nations, to establish common policies with regard to transportation, agriculture, and economic relations with non-members, and to ensure the free flow of labor and capital among member nations.

I remember Brussels from the vantage point of a toddler. We lived in a three-story Victorian house in a comfortable tree-lined neighborhood in Brussels. I loved the house with its many awkward angles, steep staircases, and cozy attic rooms. One of these attic rooms was dedicated to my brother's recreation of the Wild West, complete with green felt cloth provided by my mother, and rocks and branches from the garden for the construction of forests and hills. The other was used by guests whom we welcomed by carefully positioning cups filled with water on the door mantle, with a discreet string set to ensure that the water would pitch onto the respective guest's head when opening the door. My brothers did the engineering work while I observed their efforts with delight.

The garden was filled with huge rhododendron hedges and fir trees. The fir trees had started their career as Christmas trees, and we planted them in the yard in January. These same trees we later dug up and transported to the new garden in Bonn, where my parents were building a house. Christa wrapped the trees in bedsheets, placed them next to her onto the passenger seat of a VW beetle, and drove them to Bonn one by one. "Don't worry," she told the perplexed border guards peering into the car. "It's not my mother-in-law." Looking back on this bizarre undertaking, I suppose that my parents operated on the principle of "if you can't establish roots in a place, you take your roots with you."

My parents hosted many formal events in connection with my father's work. I liked to creep down the staircase to watch as guests arrived, anxious to catch a glimpse of my mother in her elegant black cocktail dress.

We spent hours in the kitchen where my mother outfitted us with bakers' hats and gave us tasks in the production of Christmas cookies. Agostino, already at that time adept in the kitchen, helped to mix the dough. Adrian cut out shapes when he wasn't busy taste-testing the products. My mother placed me on a little stool, handed me a fork, and poured some flour into a large bowl. "I need you to stir this." Proudly I stirred and stirred, fascinated by the clouds of flour. "Keep stirring," Christa said blithely when pretending to inspect my efforts.

Every year, Christa loaded the trunk of her VW with boxes of *Schrumpeläpfel*—small, sweet apples, so wizened they looked like tiny old grandmothers with reddened cheeks, which grew on ancient apple trees in our garden—and drove to a cider mill across the border where the apples were pressed and turned into cider.

While ferrying my brothers to judo classes and me to ballet—fortunately, my mother eventually realized that I considered ballet sheer torture and excused me from any further attempts in that direction—Christa plotted and planned the details of the house under construction in Bonn. Christa laid in a stock of textiles, fabric trims, and tassels which she used for drapes and furniture recovering. In later years, whenever I needed something for a pillow or a chair, Christa would dig in her boxes, triumphantly unearthing lovely dark red brocades and golden silks from seemingly unending supplies.

I was happy in Belgium, reveling in my status as a little girl with two older brothers. I was happy when my mother distracted us from the horrid taste of cod liver oil by reading out loud the Flemish text on the medicine bottle. Many of the Flemish words, related to Dutch and thus to German, were familiar enough that we could guess at the meaning; at the same time, we thought they sounded hilarious. I spent hours contentedly playing with a bookshelf my mother had converted into a multiple-storied dollhouse. I was happiest of all when she read to us from William Hauff's tales, *Little Long Nose*, with his wise goose Mimi, *The History of Caliph Stork*, and *The Caravan*. I was proud when my father christened a new doll presented to me at Christmas albeit puzzled by my parents' laughter about names such as Rosina Sunshine and Karl-Egon, chosen by my father. Christa refrained from enlightening me about the source of these names. Rosina Sunshine was a cabaret singer in Brussels of questionable repute, and Karl-Egon a politician whose given name my father considered irresistibly ridiculous. Christa also did not disrupt my fond belief that our kindly gardener Baudouin was the king of Belgium.

I was content and unaware of any wrinkles in the universe.

After we moved to Bonn in 1965, life became more complicated.

WU was head of the department at the international desk of the Foreign Service. That included the United Nations and other multilateral organizations. His work had increased, he had to travel regularly, and on many nights he was late.

When Christa drove us around to familiarize us with our new surroundings, she exhibited a distinct reserve about finding herself back in this small town—it was the first time that I became aware of a sense of hesitation and reluctance in her. I understood only later that in Rome and Brussels she had felt free and unencumbered by the past and reveled in a life that was anything but provincial.

My brothers and I struggled emotionally and academically, and we were old enough to be aware of my father's repeated bouts with bronchitis, aggravated by his lung condition. Entering the third grade of elementary school, I experienced for the first time the feeling of being an alien in an alien land, teased and harassed as "weird" and a "foreigner," moreover one cursed with a name distinguishing me as a member of the nobility—a handicap in Germany, at that time still painfully class-conscious. My brothers received similar treatment with the added flavor of fairly rough beatings administered by classmates. Similar challenges confronted us on the street near our house where we played with the neighbors' children. Adrian and I, then about seven and eight respectively, tried to intervene when other boys attacked Agostino, running up to them, screaming and yelling, and pummeling them with our little fists until, disgruntled and dismayed, they let go of Agostino and walked off.

Christa had perfected the art of walking into the house, still wearing her coat, starting a pot of water for pasta, cutting up vegetables, and setting out plates, before taking off her coat. She worked at great speed with enormous concentration. Once she sat down, she was calm and serene. She never got up from the dinner table until the meal was finished; instead, sending stern glances our way, she indicated that we should clear the plates and bring in whatever dishes there were for the next course.

Agostino began to copy Christa's commanding look with a raised chin and subtle hand signal and directed this toward Adrian who in turn passed it on to me—a "division of labor" among siblings later replicated when the three of us would venture into the nearby forest, where we busied ourselves with redirecting the course of streams. My oldest brother was the architect, my middle brother the engineer, and I the laborer, directed to carry rocks and branches to our construction site. It never occurred to me to question this arrangement.

At family meals, we learned the art of fielding questions.

"How was your day?"

"How was school?"

"So, you got on the bus, and then what happened?"

The questions were relentless, and we had to figure out how to handle this elegantly especially since the areas where we wanted to withhold information grew as we got older. Christa reminded us that it didn't matter so much what we told about our day or our evening out or our first date but that we learned to say something—just enough to satisfy the listener.

Our father put some of our visiting cousins through the same rigorous training or, to put it more bluntly, an inquisition.

"So, how was the party? You got picked up by Karl, and then..." my father would begin.

Our cousins, not used to this sort of thing, blushed painfully, unsure how to deflect his needling.

Of course, my father also insisted that we learn to give speeches. Every birthday offered such an opportunity. It was painful in that we knew him as the supreme master of speech-making. Christa's approach was pragmatic. "If you can't think of anything, stand up, clink the glass, and say, 'Hurrah, hurrah, hurrah.' That's good enough."

Life was predictable and steady. For the main midday meal, my father tried to be present as often as he could. Evening meals were my favorite—with bread, cold cuts, and fruit my mother would peel at the table. We ate lovely things such as pea soup, potato pancakes and apple sauce, meatloaf and mashed potatoes, "apples in nightgowns"—cut up apple pieces in dough, boiled as huge dumplings and served with browned butter, and something my mother described as "children's questions with sugar," a mess of old bread mixed with eggs and apple slices fried in a pan.

For Sunday afternoon teas, she baked bread, which was served still warm from the oven with herb butter. To my frustration, I never figured out how she did it. Sometimes she used yeast, sometimes she didn't have time to let the dough rise, and sometimes she dispensed with the yeast altogether. None of that mattered. It was always delicious, with a hard crust and a fragrant soft inside.

"Oh, I don't think about it," she said when I asked. "It's always a bit different."

I watched my mother prepare elaborate desserts for formal dinners in molds that always made me think of the ridiculous *Pickelhauben*, the pointed helmets worn by the German military, firefighters, and police in the early 1900s. I held my breath when she released the desserts from their helmet-shaped molds by opening a little valve on top that allowed the contents such as rice imperial or chocolate mousse to slide out, shape intact. When pieces broke off or remained in the mold, she never lost her cool. With a knife or anything else that came to hand, she deftly fixed the offending spots.

"It doesn't have to be perfect," she said. "No need for *rage de perfection.*"

One of her favorite expressions for this sort of thing was *überwendig*.

"We'll just do it *überwendig*," my mother would say cheerfully, without a moment's hesitation using whipped cream to paint over blemishes or adding a generous dollop of rum or sherry to a dish that she deemed to taste "like feet that have fallen asleep." By this, she meant that it tasted bland, but it is also the best description I have heard for that peculiar prickly sensation when cider is about to turn.

When trying to trace the etymology of *überwendig*, I found that it is used mainly in the medical field and refers to a so-called running stitch, made with one continuous length of suture material and used to close tissue layers. The advantages of the running stitch are speed of execution and accommodation of edema during the wound healing process.

Christa put her stamp on this word. She used it to describe something done quickly if approximately so that the surface would be presentable. The purpose was to create a good impression without aiming for perfection. This term became synonymous in my mind with her flexible approach to challenges she confronted. It allowed her to flourish in situations where others failed, incapable of adjusting to new circumstances.

When her schedule allowed, Christa liked to take brief naps in the afternoons. "Wake me up in fifteen minutes," she would tell Agostino before disappearing into her room where, like a general marshalling her forces before battle, she lay down on her back, closing her eyes and willing herself to sleep. Afterward, she made tea and resumed her day.

We spent many hours in a little room my mother used for ironing. My brothers and I did our homework to the offbeat rhythm of the thumping and groaning of the rotary machine she used to iron long linen tablecloths. Patiently she fed them into the roller and sprayed them with water. Steaming, damp, warm air filled the room with the scent of linen and starch, and I loved the hissing sound when she pressed down the iron. Occasionally she glanced at our work and responded to questions. She had a roll of wrapping paper handy with which she clunked us on the head when we made mistakes or weren't paying attention.

Homework with my father was a less comfortable experience. He was relentless in his insistence that we get it right, correcting our essays over and over again until we were ready to jump out of the window in the living room with its tantalizing and distracting view of the mountains along the Rhine.

Both my brothers and I spent a great deal of time in the riding stable. Often my mother, as well as my grandmother, would sit on the raised benches and watch us. When we fell off, their stern looks left no doubt about their expectation that we immediately get back up on the horse and continue the lesson. As a result, I once finished a lesson bemused by the fact that all the riders' white shirts had turned green; at home, it became apparent that I had a concussion. Adrian once got thrown off a bucking horse. He got up and stood on the turf, his face smudged and tears running down his cheeks. However, he mounted his horse with some difficulty and completed the lesson. He had broken his elbow.

Christa expected a lot from us and tried to instill in us the same sense of discipline and self-control that was undoubtedly instilled in her childhood. Getting back on a horse after a fall was part of that code of behavior.

This is not to imply that Christa was careless of our needs. I loved being at home when I was sick—my mother brought me hot milk and honey, placed her cool hands on my face, washed and smoothed the sheets on my bed, and read to me. In the evenings, she brushed my hair, carefully untangling the long braids, and making my skin tingle with contentment. Sometimes, when I sat next to her, she would run her fingers over the soft down of my arm, sweeping back and forth like the kisses of a butterfly. On chilly winter days in church, she let me slip my hands into the scented silken sleeves of her silver mink coat. I treasured those moments.

My parents had many guests. Throughout our years in Bonn, one or another member of Christa's first husband's family stayed with us for extended periods as did WU's nieces, other relatives, and friends. Some guests would quietly enter the house, leave their belongings in the downstairs bathroom, and go off to an event in town before reappearing at breakfast time. Another friend sauntered into the house through the garden door and slept on the sofa until teatime.

At tea, my father fed wood into the fireplace, while Christa presided over a samovar, handing out endless cups of tea and offering trays loaded with inexhaustible supplies of fresh plum tart squares. Like an experienced actor, she waited for the right cue to begin telling some of her stories. Sometimes, I prompted her, "Mima, tell the story about the sugar bowl."

With a smile at me and passing around the sugar bowl, Christa launched into the tale of a prospective mother-in-law in Muttrin. This stern lady had responded to the young bride's polite request for sugar with the acid comment, "The dessert has been sweetened." Undaunted, the young bride insisted that the servant bring her some sugar and proceeded to dump the contents of the large bowl onto her plate, effectively scotching any further attempts by said mother-in-law at controlling her.

It never bothered me that my mother may well have embellished her stories. I enjoyed that aspect just as much, intrigued to see what knot she would add to the unending string of reminiscences she spread out before our eyes.

Sitting on grey-green fieldstone slabs at the edge of the fireplace, the flames warming my back, and with a plate of plum tart on my lap, I was content. My mother's voice was my own private, magical wardrobe to another country—a country whose fascination was, if anything, enhanced by the fact that it was lost forever. It was a place where old and young were welcomed and protected, where one thought in terms of centuries rather than days, where the rules were clear, defined by values of frugality, work, and responsibility combined with generosity for those in need, and where Christa had been happy.

Road trips with my parents were memorable in that my father was convinced that stopping for bathroom breaks was entirely unnecessary. He instructed Adrian and me to sing to distract us from our urgent needs or to get over queasiness as we ascended the road to the Brenner Pass on our way to Italy. Having learned from experience that our pleas would fall on deaf ears, we sang with quavering voices and increasing desperation. He also considered stopping for food an unnecessary overindulgence.

Fortunately, my mother decided that this was taking Prussian asceticism too far. She prepared picnic baskets with sandwiches, fruit, and cookies—particularly welcome since we knew that once we arrived at my Hassell grandmother's house outside of Munich we would be served the inevitable spinach soup, risotto, and pudding, one after the other in the same chipped plate to save the cook the trouble of washing up. Admittedly, washing dishes in the huge and inconvenient slop sink from pre-World War II times in the kitchen was an imposition. My grandmother was of the firm belief that installing a proper sink or even a dishwasher was extravagant and unnecessary.

These annual pilgrimages to my paternal grandmother's house as well as to Italy to join the entire family in a run-down hotel in a small seaside town called Jesolo had all the flavor of a walk to Canossa, minus the hair shirt. In Jesolo, my parents consoled themselves with gorgonzola and copious amounts of wine, while my brothers and I would visit the hotel's kitchen to cajole the chef into feeding us with extra supplies of fresh rolls and grapes.

Christa later admitted that she was always tempted to

laugh out loud at the morning procession to the beach when we all had to follow in the wake of my Hassell grandmother, attired in a black bathing suit to signify her everlasting state of mourning and complemented by an ancient black sunhat and a black umbrella.

Our grandmother's inflexible and unforgiving insistence on frugality was hard to bear for all that we laughed about it. I will never forget her sharp comments when confronted by one of my mother's purchases or acquisitions for the house we lived in. Studying the new drapes or the refinished furniture or the china without chips in every single plate, she would raise her eyebrows. "How opulent," she would say with a sniff, disapproval radiating out of every pore. In her view, calling upon the services of a professional furniture restorer instead of resorting to glue, scotch tape, or a hammer and nails, bordered on positively sinful indulgence.

Christa rebelled against her mother-in-law's judgmental attitude and chose to ignore it. She felt compelled to maintain her surroundings in a way that showed her respect for the items she had managed to retain throughout the war. She believed that she held them in trust. That meant that everything was cared for, polished, and repaired in as professional a manner as possible. At the same time, she never lost her ability to do without when necessary.

Meanwhile, my Studnitz grandmother's unpredictable and frightening rages inspired Christa to make a conscious decision to never lose her self-control as a parent. Admirable as such self-control was, at times I would have found it easier if she had occasionally lost her temper with us. Instead, we were never in any doubt when she was angry, but she did not give voice to it. However, she suffered from migraines, and these felt like a punishment of a different sort.

Christa's migraines were debilitating, generally lasted two or three days, and put everything on hold. Most importantly, they affected my father's outlook on life. Exuding unhappiness, he would make inept moves to take over the kitchen and to our dismay had a bizarre facility for locating all the spoiled food in the refrigerator. He insisted that it had to be consumed since tossing out food or pouring milk down the drain was unacceptable. The relief I felt when my mother resurfaced was indescribable.

These migraines were worst at the beginning of the new year, around the dates of her brother's and her father's death on January 10, 1943 and January 13, 1943 respectively.

As children, my brothers and I were familiar with her reaction when the doorbell happened to ring. She froze, her entire body language communicating hostile rejection. Only as an adult, I began to understand how her experiences during the war and its aftermath had left indelible scars. An unexpected person outside the front door meant bad news, a telegram announcing yet another death, or a house search by the occupying army.

Friends asked me whether my parents were very strict. I can't say that they were; in many respects, they were tolerant and relaxed and for their generation remarkably liberal. On the other hand, we didn't have any leeway when it came to choices. Things were done the way my parents decided, and no argument was possible.

My father's strictness was hidden underneath a calm manner; it was nearly impossible to provoke him into outbursts of anger. Most annoying for us as children was his insistence on rational arguments and logic and on ensuring that we understood the reasoning behind a decision or consequence. My father's dominance had an almost lawyerly flair. He was always willing to debate with us indefinitely, but we never could win such a debate. His arguments were cogent and flawless, which, of course, made them even more infuriating.

Christa was definite in her expectations, and when she wanted something, she expressed this in such a way that we were in no doubt whatsoever. She ruled by sheer willpower. Saying no was not an option.

In later years, we would tease Christa by saying that in her way of thinking "control" was always written with a capital C.

My brothers and I pushed and rebelled against this in different ways and devised strategies of response. One response was to hide one's cards as a way to avoid getting in trouble. Another was to assume the role of the one that is lazy, simply refusing to move actually and metaphorically speaking. I preferred to go with the flow and stay under the radar.

My parents observed a strict rule of never discussing problems with outsiders. Any issues concerning us were kept entirely within the family. Consciously this was to protect us, but on another level, I suspect it helped Christa to retain a modicum of control. If something was not public knowledge, it was more manageable. This habit of utmost discretion also extended to limited open discussion among us about troubling matters, e.g., an illness that landed me in a hospital for months at a time, school challenges confronted by one brother, and emotional challenges confronted by another. We all knew of each other's struggles, but nothing was said aloud.

Several times, Christa was away from home for months at a time due to recurring bouts of illness related to her liver issues. She spent time in a hospital and also in Italy to recuperate. This was not explained to us. I missed her dreadfully, and the presence of my grandmother in those times was not adequate consolation.

My father would ask us to write to Christa, allotting to each of us space on a skinny blue airmail sheet, and the length of our respective communications was in direct reflection of our eagerness to write—the older the child, the shorter the missive. On the back, my father added his commentary, laughing at our efforts and describing what we were doing so that Christa could see it all in front of her.

In my letters, I engaged in lengthy descriptions of my

efforts to convince a horse to jump over a small obstacle and admitted to falling off but stated triumphantly that I was on a fair way to matching my "big" brothers' performance. This "big" in quotation marks indicated both my acknowledgement that I would not be likely to match their riding skills for a long time to come but that I also found it funny to be in a position of having to look up to my "big" brothers. I reported that a visiting aunt had insisted on "appropriate behavior" which involved what we called "scraping and bowing," assured that Christa would be amused. With that same ironic detachment, I wrote to my father that I had added elements to a school essay, in my wording as "freely adapted by Malve," a euphemism for simply making stuff up.

Endearingly, Adrian wrote that he had earned an F and a D on math tests, following this up with the comment, "but I think I did better than the last time." In an attempt at impression management, he reported that his girth had been measured by our grandmother, a painful bone of contention for him as he struggled with his weight for many years. "I lost two centimeters." He signed this letter, "with respectful wishes from your "thin" (his quotation marks) *Dickmops*." "Dickmops," literally a roly-poly, was our parents' nickname for my brother.

In my father's letters, silence and layers of distance appeared in the form of a curious stiff formality—his writing style was informed by his legal training as much as by his detachment and skepticism. In his letters to his brother, he always addressed him as "My dear brother." My brothers and I sometimes aped this tone as a way to make fun of my father and ourselves. For instance, Adrian ended some of his letters to Christa with "your dear son."

In our childhood, we acquired the family habit of speaking elliptically. We enjoyed our cryptic form of communication. It set us apart and even served as a way to test unfortunate outsiders and to give us yet another reason to distance ourselves.

WU's language usage was littered with irony and cryptic references. For instance, when he wanted to describe someone as having a weak character, a shirker who preferred to hide behind another, he simply used the name *Leubelfing*. This name comes from a novella by Conrad Ferdinand Meyer, "Gustav Adolf's Page." The lead character is Gustl, a girl whose cousin Anton Leubelfing is appalled to be called upon to serve as a page to King Gustav Adolf of Sweden during the Thirty Years War, a position known for being precarious at best. Pages were expected to stay close to the king in battle and were the first to attract the enemy's fire. The girl, unswayed by the long list of pages, who had already paid for the honor of serving the king by being killed in battle, decides to take on the role herself. She disguises herself as a boy and serves as a page. Eventually, she dies at the king's side. I adored this book, and when my father referred to someone in his acquaintance as a *Leubelfing*, I immediately knew what he meant.

He taught us the term *Conte Pinco Pallino*. Derived from the Italian version of 'Count John Doe,' this meant someone who sported a title and thought of himself as important but was, in reality, a nobody, an inflated little person of no significance. We did not need any explanation and also were aware of my father's casual disdain for titles, for all that it was part of the world in which he had grown up.

From our father we also picked up an appreciation for a characteristic in the German language that facilitates a form of speech described as *doppelbödig*, poorly if correctly translated as ambiguous. *Doppelbödig* refers to a structure with two floorings, one installed above each other, with a hollow space in between. Hence, a *doppelbödig* form of language usage, with its multiple layers of meaning, evokes the notion of walking on uncertain ground that may crack open and pitch you into a lower level.

Years of Nazi rule had a profound impact on the German language and lent this facility for double-speak or ambiguity an additional layer of complexity. Victor Klemperer, a renowned scholar and writer, described how the Nazi era had perverted the impact of formerly innocuous words like mother, father, loyalty, truth, honor, faith, home, country, and countless others to the point that those who had lived through those years would always stumble over them, unable to shake the unwanted association like a bitter taste on the tongue or a stench one can't forget. For people of my parents' generation as well as the next one, the very act of speaking was filled with emotional minefields. My father recommended Klemperer's book to me. "There is nothing the Nazis haven't managed to stain," he said with an expression of helpless despondency.

Christa reacted reflexively when confronted with particular terms. The word "Mother's Day" is a case in point. When I was about three years old, a nanny helped me to collect wildflowers and told me I should present the bouquet to my mother for Mother's Day. I don't remember what Christa said at the time. Her rejection must have been more than explicit. I never dared to do that again; however, it wasn't until much later that I began to understand why.

The Nazis certainly didn't invent Mother's Day. In one form or another, it had already existed as a venerable tradition in many countries. However, during the 1930s, this day became indelibly linked with notions of women bearing children for their *Führer*. It was declared a national holiday, and women were awarded medals for bearing children.

Christa's self-control was paramount, and she and my father presented a united front in their interactions with us. Calling my parents strict would be too simplistic a term. They were dominant by sheer force of character.

Thus, while we were growing up, life presented us with a perplexing mix of exertion of absolute control, my mother's occasional absences due to migraines or sickness, a veil of silence that was nearly impenetrable, and animated storytelling that we loved.

Looking back on the hours spent listening to my mother weave entire worlds for us with her words, I wonder to what extent her vivid storytelling was a form of retreat behind an invisible barrier, a mask of sorts that disguised the degree to which many things were never spoken about. Yet, those unspoken realms, whether regarding the losses of the past or present fears and concerns, were always present, lurking in the background—hidden fault lines only occasionally hinted at. We knew of them, but also feared that asking questions might not only fail in getting an answer but might also disturb the enchantment emanating from her stories.

Only once in my childhood did my mother lose her self-control. At the time, I had only a vague understanding of what had happened, although I was moved by the image of Chancellor Willy Brandt laying down a wreath at the monument in memory of the victims of the Warsaw Ghetto and spontaneously kneeling, with his dark winter coat draped around him.

On that same day, December 7, 1970, Willy Brandt signed the Treaty of Moscow, renouncing the use of force and recognizing the European borders drawn up after World War II. He followed this up by signing a treaty with Poland at the same time. The Treaty of Warsaw formally recognized the People's Republic of Poland and reiterated the Federal Republic's recognition of the Oder–Neisse line and the current borders, thereby putting an end to long-standing disputes. It meant that Christa's childhood home in Pomerania was now officially and definitively part of another country. In practice, this had been so since 1945, but for Christa, the final formal recognition of this reality was a devastating blow.

My parents talked about this at dinner, while my brothers and I listened, helpless and shocked at the raw emotions. I remember my mother's flushed face, her eyes swollen, and her voice shaky. I also recall my father's calm responses, laying out the political rationale and the utter necessity of this step by Willy Brandt.

"You can't turn back the clock," he said.

"You don't understand. You weren't born there," Christa kept repeating, swaying back and forth as if the motion could make it all disappear like a bad dream.

I suppose WU didn't understand. He came from a line of bureaucrats, minor government officials, and officers, and the only property with some land attached to it had been gambled away by a reckless ancestor. He did not have Christa's bone-deep attachment to the land of her birth and the attendant faith in continuity from generation to generation. In this respect, if not in others, WU belonged in the 20th century, defined by fluid boundaries, mobility, and rootlessness.

For Christa, Pomerania was home. It had nothing to do with the ideology pushed by the Nazis according to which Prussia and East Prussia had been an intrinsic part of what was considered essentially German and referenced with the concept of "blood and soil."

Perhaps I remember this day so distinctly because afterward there was no further discussion of it. Christa as always when confronted with an unalterable fact swallowed and moved on, returning to business as usual. The loss and grief were buried deep inside of her.

In the fall of 1971, my father was promoted to assume the position of second in command at the German Mission to the United Nations in New York City.

10

ACTE DE PRESENCE

CHRISTA AND I ARRIVED IN NEW YORK CITY ON A BITTERLY cold January evening in 1972, joining my father who had already started in his new position in the fall.

Agostino and Adrian were to stay in Germany for the time being. Agostino was embarking on his first year at university. Adrian had just two years left of high school, and my parents decided that it would be better for him if he didn't have to switch schools at that point. They arranged for housing for him in a nearby boarding school.

I was looking forward to New York and very happy to escape from a high school where teachers played favorites with abandon while my attempts at friendship with girls in my class, all older than I by one or two years, led to failure if not outright derision.

Only many years later Christa admitted to me how much she had grieved at the time to leave her sons behind and how afraid she had been of New York. I had no idea of this when I sat next to her in the airplane, quivering with excitement.

Christa was then forty-nine, and I was fourteen. Bemused, we stared at endless streams of lights when we circled above JFK, only later understanding that this was Queens. Christa took everything in with avid eyes. Typical for her, she had read up on New York City and confounded my father's driver by asking him why he used the Triboro Bridge instead of the Queensboro Bridge. It turned out that she was right; since we were going to the hotel on 39th Street and Lexington Avenue where my father had been staying, taking the Queensboro Bridge would have been better. She was only momentarily chastened when informed that what she considered a possible area for looking for an apartment was the block of buildings associated with Rikers Island.

Christa loved New York City. Undeterred by the bitter cold of our first winter, she walked everywhere. She laughed at the chaos and the confusion and was amused by the steam pouring out of holes in the streets, with garbage cans placed on top as a warning to drivers so that they knew to avoid them. She befriended fruit vendors at street corners and deli owners where we bought our newspaper. She began to explore the galleries and museums, and it took her very little time to know her way around.

We ended up staying in that hotel for about four months. It was difficult to find an apartment in New York City. Diplomats had a reputation for not paying their rent in addition to hosting too many parties. The German government granted my father a subsidy for housing; however, that would stretch only so far. My father wanted to stay in Manhattan since it would be easier. He would be expected to attend as well as host many social functions. My father finally was able to rent an apartment on Park Avenue in the eighties.

In the first year, Christa made a point of picking me up from the bus stop after school every afternoon. I appreciated this, feeling adrift in the big city and without friends beyond the school environment. I remember looking out of the First Avenue bus, hoping I could already see my mother at the street corner, with our dog in tow.

Perversely, after years of having pleaded for a dog, my

parents finally allowed me to have one once we settled in our apartment, a decision they explained by their concern that I was lonely and didn't yet have any friends in the city. Every day I would walk around with our cocker spaniel. Since we lived just a few blocks from Central Park, I quickly became familiar with all the walkways and paths through the woods. One day, coming out of the ramble, I encountered a flasher. At first, I was stunned; then I gripped the leash tighter and walked away as quickly as I could. Meanwhile, I did not mention this to my parents. In retrospect, I wonder why this was so. When I thought about it, I concluded it was just sad and grimy rather than frightening. Perhaps I didn't want to have them put an end to my solitary walks in Central Park. In any event, we never talked about it just as we never talked about many things.

My father assumed his duties in New York at a pivotal time. The Federal Republic of Germany (West Germany or FRG) had been admitted to the UN as an observer in 1955. The German Democratic Republic (East Germany or GDR) was admitted as an observer in 1972. So, there were effectively two Germanies vying for full membership in the United Nations. On September 18, 1973, both were admitted as full members by the United Nations General Assembly. For diplomats like my father, it presented a challenging conundrum. Any interactions with representatives of the GDR had to be handled with care, sensitivity, and respect, while the FRG was also intent on smoothing the path to a hoped-for eventual reunification of the divided country.

My father's higher diplomatic rank as ambassador and deputy head of the German Mission to the United Nations came with increased demands on Christa's time.

"Important exchanges don't happen at formal meetings," my father explained to me.

"They happen in hallways." Diplomacy was as much about symbolic statements and formal negotiations between representatives as it was about informal, relaxed exchanges, and the creation of relationships between individuals. He considered the innumerable dinners, luncheons, and cocktails hosted or attended by him and Christa a vital part of his active duty as a representative of his country.

Christa was in charge of the organization and preparation of all these functions. She reveled in this task, embracing it with enthusiasm combined with professionalism and flexible ingenuity, managing to stay within a tight budget dictated by the German foreign office by drawing on all her skills of organizing, planning, and cooking. Throughout the years of my father's tenure, Christa maintained a log in which she recorded the menus, decorations, and seating charts for each event, making sure that she never repeated herself. Based on this record, WU and Christa entertained over 3,500 people in New York City in five years.

Once, when there was a city-wide blackout in the middle of a dinner party, she served the dessert and then sent the guests down the twelve stories, one after the other like choirboys, carrying candles in the darkened stairwell. She received glowing accolades from her guests for months after that evening.

"When you go to a party, you need to work at it if you want to have a good time," Christa said. She applied this same maxim to her parties, playing tag team with my father to make sure that everyone was having a good time.

As an adult, I sometimes witnessed how my parents would split up and proceed to work the room. Afterward, they talked about the people they had met in a form of debriefing or "maneuver review." My parents used this same military expression to describe their habit of analyzing any event hosted by them and trying to determine what they could have done better. They did this to us as well when we began hosting parties; this was as funny and entertaining as it was deeply annoying, most especially when their criticism was justified.

Christa prepared all dinners down to the last detail. When she was finished, she changed into elegant evening wear in a matter of minutes and welcomed James the butler who worked at all my parents' formal functions from 1972 until 1978. She gave him her instructions to be passed on to the kitchen staff—"this needs to be heated, here is the main course, here is the parsley for the potatoes..." delivered at top speed, and then said with a big smile, "I am off to a cocktail party at Ambassador XYZ's residence, but it's just an *acte de presence*. I'll be back at 7:30."

Often, she attended several functions before hosting a dinner at home, smoothly

weaving in and out of a crowd, making sure her presence had been noted, and departing in a flawless performance of an *acte de presence*.

Christa's duties included entertaining spouses of visiting German dignitaries as well as attending informational events and tours together with other spouses from the diplomatic community such as visits to educational institutions, shelters, and the justice system. She was fascinated by these glimpses into life in America and New York City.

Christa's health issues caught up with her in the mid-1970s. She was hospitalized and had to undergo a hysterectomy. I was able to piece this together only after the fact. After a brief period of recuperation, Christa returned home, and it was business as usual.

In those same years, Christa went back to school. She signed up for graduate courses at New York University's Institute of Fine Arts, reimmersing herself in her original field of study. Sometimes, in a role reversal, while I was still living at home during my last year in high school, I would pick her up at the institute, which was not far from our apartment. She would walk out the door, chatting with some of the younger students and beaming at me when she saw me. In retrospect, it is clear that Christa was already preparing for her life after my father's retirement.

By the time I graduated from high school and was about to leave for college, both my brothers had joined us in America. Adrian worked at a law firm for a few years after college and then went to law school in Tennessee. Agostino earned a master's degree in journalism before starting his career as a journalist.

WU and Christa gradually came to realize that remaining in New York City would suit them; their decision was supported by the fact that my brothers and I had all studied in America and were embarking on a life in this country. For my parents, being outsiders in a city and a country where many are by definition outsiders seemed far more palatable than being outsiders in a country that is in theory one's home. They never forgot their appreciation of a country that allowed them their history without defining them by it.

Christa loved the landscape on the South Fork of Long Island, where we had spent several summers in rental cottages. She would be grieved to know that there are hardly any potato fields left. In the 1970s, the area was still quite rural in parts. When Christa heard of a plot of land for sale in Southampton, she didn't hesitate and convinced WU to make an offer. On this same plot of land, my parents built a small weekend house based on Christa's drawings that were fine-tuned with the help of a contractor.

"You can't do that," the contractor told Christa when she asked about a fireplace in a loft space.

"Oh, yes, you can," she said cheerfully, whipping out a sketch. "This is how."

In 1978, my parents were getting ready for retirement. Always quick to scent out a good deal, Christa heard of an apartment on 57th Street that had been on the market for a long time, largely because the seller had difficulty in finding a buyer who was able to produce a sufficient number of references for the finicky board of the building. As it happened, my parents knew several parties in the building as a result of my father's work as a diplomat. My father, as usual, hesitated, worried about making too quick a decision; however, Christa convinced him. Armed with stellar credentials if not a large portfolio, Christa made a low bid, and the apartment became my parents' home.

Moving out of the apartment my father had used as a diplomat occurred in two legs; one truck went to the new apartment, and another went to the new weekend house. My father went to the apartment, and I accompanied my mother.

It was raining when the truck arrived in Southampton in the later afternoon. Christa had prepared a large pot of soup that she had transported in our car, precariously wrapped with plastic bags and string tied around the top, so it wouldn't spill. She had also brought a set of soup plates and spoons as well as a loaf of fresh bread. Once the truck was unloaded and boxes stood all over the house, the movers sat on the staircase for lack of furniture. Like pigeons arranged on a branch, they contentedly ate their soup.

"This has never happened to us before," one mover said when getting ready to leave. "We won't forget this move."

That night, a portion of the basement flooded. I later discovered that this was due to a faulty dry well in combination with a sea of mud without landscaping around the house. I hurried into my mother's bedroom to report this. However, three inches of water in the basement were not enough to upset her balance. She had achieved her goal, a new place to put down roots. She laughed, turned over, and went to sleep.

❧ 11 ❧

RESIDENT ALIEN

AFTER MY FATHER'S RETIREMENT IN 1978, CHRISTA metaphorically brushed off her hands, straightened her back, and plunged into her next venture, once again as so many times before reinventing herself.

Meanwhile, my parents, my brothers, and I needed to apply for green cards. Until that point, we had had diplomatic passports with extended stay visas. Our work permits remained in place while the application process was winding its way through the system. It took five years, with several hitches. Adrian's and my applications were rejected and sent to Italy for processing. Since we were both born in Italy, INS had concluded that we were Italian citizens. It took over a year to retrieve our original documents. Several interviews at INS bordered on the Kafkaesque in that the examiner assigned to our case insisted that Christa produce a death certificate for her first husband. Since her first husband had died in a prisoner-of-war camp in Russia, such a death certificate did not exist. The examiner also held up proceedings for several months over my father's birth certificate. He was born in Italy in 1913, and the original birth certificate made out in Genoa was lost. The examiner insisted that my father produce additional testimony from his mother or father, both unsurprisingly long deceased.

These hitches were funny albeit infuriating. They also made us painfully aware of how privileged we were in being able to hire an attorney and to be able to communicate in English. It was profoundly humbling and moving to sit in one of the large waiting halls in Federal Plaza with other applicants for green cards or citizenship, many of whom looked desperate and overwhelmed. Compared to the challenges they had to contend with, the restriction on travel abroad for the duration of our open application was a minor inconvenience. However, it was an enormous relief when the green cards identifying us as resident aliens finally arrived about five years after we had started the process.

Christa started to work as a reporter for a German monthly publication, *Weltkunst*, also submitting regular columns to *Die Welt*. She reported about the art market in New York and particular exhibits as well as galleries, old and new. She attended auctions at Sotheby's, Philips, and Christie's, among others. Occasionally she wrote feature pieces about a particular artist who had appeared on the art scene in New York. She was thrilled when the Neue Galerie opened in 2001, a museum of early twentieth-century German and Austrian art and design, and the house in Southampton was filled with posters showing works by Wassily Kandinsky, Paul Klee, Ernst Ludwig Kirchner, Lyonel Feininger, Otto Dix, Gustav Klimt, and George Grosz, among others. She expanded her knowledge about modern art and also delved into completely new territories; for instance, she was friends with an expert on Asian art and made use of every opportunity to learn more about it.

She went all over the city, like a typical New Yorker often preferring to walk because she thought she'd reach her goal more quickly. Coming home, she would enthusiastically describe everything she had seen before disappearing in the cubbyhole that served as her office. She wrote her reports on a small typewriter and faxed them to Germany. Her fax machine was an old model with shiny curling paper. After several years of this maddening insistence on frugality, Adrian and I managed to convince her to invest in a better machine to simplify her life. Eventually, she graduated to a little computer, although by unspoken agreement Adrian and I decided that introducing Christa to the Internet would be begging for trouble, terrified by the challenges of trying to steer her past all the potential scams not to mention dealing with her habit of clicking on everything in sight.

As it was, Adrian was called on to troubleshoot almost every day. When she couldn't reach him, it was my turn.

"Malve, I don't know what to do," she said when I picked up the phone. "I have these funny signs on my screen, and I can't find the auction report I wrote." She insisted on saving documents under the generic file name Y. She thought that meant "YES, I am saving the document." Such calls resulted in hilarious exchanges about the significance of the terms "to close" a document or to "exit" the screen.

"Should I unplug the computer?" she asked hopefully.

She persevered despite the challenges involved, and the product of her labors was invariable flawless when she faxed it to Germany. She learned to fit the auction reports into the strict parameters dictated by the publisher and to include all salient points despite a limited word count. Her reports and her articles were succinct and with a sharp sense of humor that made them entertaining as well as informative.

For several years, she acted as a consultant to a German antique furniture dealer who was just getting started in New York City. She helped him with contacts and made many suggestions regarding the design and setup of his store. She also wrote several articles about his collection of Biedermeier furniture.

Initially, WU was eager to look at Christa's writing before

she sent it out. However, she quickly put a stop to that, complaining to me that she would never get anything done in that way since my father was relentless when it came to editing.

Indeed, WU's colleagues at the German embassy had framed the cover of a report and presented this to him at his retirement party. On the top of the report, a colleague had written, "What, Dr. von Hassell, were you not feeling well? You signed off on this without a single correction."

Amused, but unrepentant, WU's response was "I was pleased to see that after thirty-two revisions, the report was finally in good order."

For Christa to have my father look over her work was unsustainable. Hurt, he retreated to his library.

The first years after WU's retirement proved to be a challenge. The combination of strenuous work at the German embassy to the United Nations, worries about my brothers and me, and the ongoing struggle with asthma had taken an enormous toll on my father. He spent much of his time at home, struggling with a lack of energy and depression while waiting for Christa to return and laboriously preparing tea for her. At times, WU was so trapped in his misery that it was as if fog surrounded him as he sat at his desk, lost amidst stacks of paperwork and books he was planning to read.

Christa, glowing and elated with her work and her new world to conquer, dealt with my father's depression by ignoring it for the most part or at times trying to laugh him out of his corner of misery. My brothers and I engaged in all sorts of ultimately fruitless interventions. Perhaps Christa was right; eventually, after a period of rest and reflection over several years, my father regained his balance and settled into his new life.

I was still living at home. I was twenty-one and in graduate school, enrolled in a Ph.D. program in anthropology at the New School for Social Research. Watching my father struggle with his depression while Christa engaged in a whirl of activity, I often felt as if I was choking. Ironically, it was as if I had taken my father's problems with getting enough air through his scarred lung tissue into myself. I was turning into a bizarre mirror image of my father after years of worrying and waiting for his labored breath whenever there was a stressful situation. I decided that I needed to move out.

After a lengthy search, I found an apartment that I could afford on my salary at the time. I was working in various low-level office jobs and had also begun teaching German in a language school at little more than minimum wage, but it provided me with a modicum of independence while attending courses. However, my credit rating was insufficient, and I needed my parents' signature on the lease. This led to my biggest fight with my mother, a no-holds-barred furious conflagration.

I understood Christa's objections—the apartment on 81st Street between York Avenue and First Avenue was a railroad apartment on the ground floor in a derelict walkup, with nothing but a rickety front door between me and the outside world. Meanwhile, even in the heat of the battle, I dimly realized that in addition to her reasonable concerns about my safety, Christa felt bereft and abandoned. I was the last child to leave home, and I was doing so at a time when my father was trapped in a deep, dark tunnel of depression.

Eventually, Christa relented. Like a good general she realized that her position on the battlefield could not be held. The discussion was over, and I moved out.

In retrospect, it is easier to understand what lay beneath her intense and unyielding opposition. Faced with a situation she could not control, she reverted to the survivor skills acquired in her youth and during World War II. Her experiences had magnified her determination never to give in or to give up, never to admit to any doubt, and to fight back when challenged. She learned to keep her cards to herself and to stay silent. When confronted by a threat—real or perceived, she hid her fear behind an aggressive stance, retreating into icy silence. These survivor skills had served her well in times of war and the experience of intense losses, hunger, deprivation, and fear. They became a two-edged sword once those times were over.

Infinitely wise and perceptive about other people, she reacted like a frightened hedgehog, figuratively drawing in her head, and displaying her stiffened spines, when anyone tried to enter her realm with intrusive questions or anything verging on criticism. Nor could she ever say, "I was wrong," or "I am afraid," or "I am sorry." In her internal code, which held a firm grip on her emotions, any such admission would have been equivalent to a loss of control.

Learning to be my own person was a painful process. Even once I had removed myself from the immediate impact of the world of my parents, it still threatened to subsume and overwhelm my own life. I couldn't distinguish the shadows of the past from the shadows of my own making. I struggled to distance myself by reducing my visits home, at times even engaging in ludicrous strategies such as disconnecting my phone. My mother's presents—invariably tasteful, thoughtful, imaginative, and perfect—evoked feelings of helpless rejection and anger, especially when she decided to place them into my apartment in my absence as a loving surprise. She knew what I would like and refused to accept any boundaries I might try to establish.

While in graduate school, I read an essay by Walter Benjamin that resonated with me.

"A Klee painting named 'Angelus Novus' shows an angel looking as though he is about to move away from something he is fixedly contemplating. His eyes are staring, his mouth is open, his wings are spread. This is how one pictures the angel of history. His face is turned toward the past. Where we perceive a chain of events, he sees one single catastrophe which keeps piling wreckage and hurls it in front of his feet. The angel would like to stay, awaken the dead, and make whole what has been smashed. But a storm is blowing in from Paradise; it has got caught in his wings with such violence that the angel can no longer close them. The storm irresistibly propels him into the future to which his back is turned, while the pile of debris before him grows skyward. This storm is what we call progress." (Benjamin, 1969: 249).

Of course, it was utterly presumptuous that I should think of appropriating this image and projecting it onto my own life, but I did it anyway. Born in 1957, I saw life through the lens of parents who had experienced the utter moral and physical devastation of their country. It shaped the way I thought and felt even while I fought against that, struggling to distinguish between their world and my own.

In my first years of living on my own, I veered back and forth between exhilaration about my independence and utter despondency and uncertainty, leavened by a goodly amount of young adult angst in search of the meaning of existence.

I spent a great deal of time listening to Leonard Cohen, whose perplexing lyrics, delivered in a voice redolent with smoke and sweat, like a Rorschach test were endlessly malleable to my moods, and singing along with Toto's "Africa," craving the sounds of rain starting on the plain and the wild dogs howling in the dark. Like B. Hayden in John le Carré's *Tinker, Tailor, Soldier, Spy*, I felt the urge to go outside in desperate search of someone—anyone at all—to escape from the feeling that the walls were caving in. The apartment was a haven as much as a hiding place where I struggled with being lonely and craving solitude all at the same time.

Gradually, I began to discover a life unexpected.

My apartment was certainly questionable, and during my tenure, there were three break-ins. But it was mine in all its battered glory, patched up, filled with street furniture, and enhanced by the noises of odd neighbors in the basement space whose lights I could see through the floorboards. Who gets to live above a Chinese laundry, followed by a shady car service agency, followed by a Chinese takeout, the scents of which pervaded my apartment, and finally by an elderly couple selling Civil War paraphernalia and unsynchronized cuckoo clocks that entertained me at night? I loved my neighbors, in particular, the wobbly old ladies who took care of the geraniums in tiny pots on top of the banister. I loved the neighborhood with its Hungarian bakeries and small street corner shops. Much of that is now gone.

I loved my kitchen bathtub with its distinctive cast-iron feet. It doubled as my buffet table for parties, and I treasured the days when a friend of mine, whose apartment building often shut off the warm water, appeared at my door. "Can I take a bath?" he asked. He would sit in a cloud of soap bubbles and steam with his eyes closed, listening to Beethoven's Fidelio on the radio next to the tub, while I prepared dinner.

One night was particularly memorable. A basement boiler in the walkup next door exploded and blew out the windows of the apartment building across the street. I sat on the stoop in my pajamas, talking to other people spilling out onto the sidewalk, and vastly entertained by the story of the landlord who used to fix this same boiler by plugging a dowel wrapped in a rag into one of its holes.

One of my jobs while in graduate school was teaching German. It was the worst paid job I ever had and in retrospect also one of the most worthwhile in my odd collection of employment situations, which included, among others, a stint in a greeting card factory. Painfully shy and lacking self-confidence, I usually aimed low when looking for work, trying not to move too far out of my comfort zone. Teaching German at rates that did not exceed minimum wage and with unpredictable hours and certainly without any benefits seemed in my reach. To my surprise, I found that I could do it well and that I enjoyed it. This confidence later translated into other jobs.

My thesis advisor in graduate school suggested that for my dissertation research I should focus on a history of the New School for Social Research, the so-called University in Exile, which in the 1930s had become a haven for scholars whose careers and lives were threatened by the Nazis. My advisor thought that I would be well equipped to write about it from my perspective as a German, moreover one whose family was associated with the resistance movement against Hitler. Appalled and shaken, I mumbled something about not having the proper detachment for such a monumental task and declined.

It was the only possible decision for me at the time and not only because of serious doubts on my part about my ability to handle such a complex topic well. Immersing myself in the history of the New School and by the same token in the history of Germany was the last thing I wanted to do.

Preferring to venture farther afield, my dissertation focused on the first generation of Japanese immigrant women in America and their relationship with their daughters. The research taught me a lot about the shadowlands of protective and defensive forms of communication between generations. As part of this work, I studied Japanese. I explored New York City. I discovered entire worlds in books, surprising, thrilling, and entirely unrelated to anything I had ever read before.

Most importantly, I came upon moments of grace.

Running rapids on a river was one. A lucky coincidence resulted in a job where I acted as a general gofer on travels throughout the United States. One of these trips included a three-day river rafting excursion on the Green River in Utah. Running rapids can be a frightening experience when you have no experience of anything like it. For minutes at a time, you have no time to think, deafened by the roaring of the water as your raft is swept downstream, leaping up and down on the waves, and hurled around eddies and treacherous rocks. And then, as if someone had waved a magic wand, you slide into a patch of calm water below the rapids. That moment of exquisite stillness is an experience like no other, and it opened worlds for me.

Another such moment fills me with exhilaration to this day. The first major snowstorm of the season had begun during the evening hours, and a silvery, muffled silence settled on the dark city streets. I lived within walking distance of Central Park, and something inspired me to pull on my winter gear and venture outside. There was no traffic, and the street-lamps shimmered in veils of drifting flakes. By the time I reached the park, it had stopped snowing. Everything was coated by pristine, glittering blankets of snow. Other people must have had the same idea, flooding into the park from all directions. As I trudged through the snow, creating my own footprints upon the world, and marveling at the transformed landscape, I listened to voices in the dark, laughing and calling out to each other in their excitement. I was alone, and yet I felt connected to all the people around me.

There were other such moments. However, the most important one was not linked to any particular external event or activity.

I remember the moment as if it happened yesterday.

During the last year of my graduate school studies, I worked in the development office at Columbia University as an office assistant. It was a windy day in October after a dry, hot summer, and many trees had already begun to shed their leaves. On my way home, I entered the subway station on 116th Street. A downtown train was on the platform with the doors open. Followed by wind sweeping around the corners of the staircase onto the platform, I entered the nearly empty wagon. There was a hold up somewhere down the line, and the train stood on the platform for several minutes with the doors open, the only sounds the whistling of the conductor, low voices of people talking after a long day of work, the screeching of the turnstiles, and the clicking of tokens as they were plugged into their slots. I was tired, my mind a blank, holding on to the metal bar, trying to decide whether I should sit down when I saw it.

A miniature lion—golden red and brown, the ruff around its head trembling and with a toothless grin all over its broad snout. Perhaps it was a second, maybe it was minutes or an eternity. Then I lost my focus, and with a shiver it was gone from the platform, leaving nothing but a pile of dried leaves and debris in its wake.

It made me happy all the way home.

It was my lion. It didn't matter that it never existed. It had been alive at that moment, as real as anything I had ever seen. It has stayed with me to this day, trembling and smiling, and entirely my own.

This moment, insubstantial, nothing but a puff of air, and gone in a blink of the eye, became a key for finding joy, a key I mislaid sometimes in the years to come but always found again. Those moments of grace—happiness is the wrong word for it, too narrowly defined—are the building bricks for one's ability to achieve contentment, and they are not dependent on external factors. They come from inside.

Ultimately it led me back to Christa, whose ability to be open to such moments was astounding. She found joy in the littlest things that life offers.

As I gained more confidence and developed my own passions, my relationship with my mother underwent a subtle transformation from daughter to friend and ally. Christa was fascinated by my enthusiasm about my graduate school studies and at my request joined me for several lectures with a professor whom I admired. With an open mind and open heart, she went to gallery shows of an artist with whom I was in love. She gave me more space.

Visiting museums with Christa was an unforgettable experience. She never missed an opportunity to teach and to point out things she did not want me to miss, such as the fact that Gainsborough used broccoli trees as models for his landscape paintings. Whenever we visited an exhibition, we played a game. "You can take one painting home with you," Christa said when we entered a gallery, fixing me with a stern look on her face. "Which one will it be?" It forced me to focus and to choose.

Working as an art reporter, Christa with a magpie-like industry began forming relationships with dealers, auctioneers, and art experts all over New York City. Regularly she and WU would host dinners for old and new acquaintances and friends. Operating with a shoestring budget, she purchased meat and fish at various markets on the West Side, located obscure sources for vegetables and fruit, and prepared countless dishes with an inventive and joyful spirit.

"When you want to prepare a decent meal, you have two choices," she told me. "You can choose to spend a lot of money, or you work hard and take your time." She worked hard.

My brothers and I dubbed some of the new friends who washed up on the shores of Christa's court "the European orphans." They were taken in, dried off, fed a decent meal, and handed a glass of wine, while they were subjected to Christa's inquisition mixed with explicit and firm instructions on what they needed to do to make their stay in New York City a success. They became part of an expanding orbit.

In those years, I began to appreciate the vast network of friends, family, and acquaintances that my parents had built up over the years. It extended backward in time to the years before World War II; it reached across many countries, in part due to the respective young adult years of both my parents and in part because of my father's career as a diplomat. Some friendships were rooted in shared experiences during and after the war, some in a shared history, class, culture, and education. Throughout their lives, both WU and Christa returned to those friendships like batteries in need of recharging, but they kept expanding their circle with an open and inquisitive attitude toward all people they encountered.

This included the friends we brought home—at times to our frustration.

"Why does Mima always have to take over my girlfriends," Adrian complained to me repeatedly. "They end up liking her more than me."

"What is it like to grow up with perfect parents?" Michael, a close friend of Christa's and frequent visitor at my parents' summer home, asked me one afternoon. We were standing in the garden, and out of the corner of my eye, I watched Christa preparing tea on the porch with her usual energy and cheerfulness.

I laughed, trying to hide my sense of discomfort with this question. Michael was teasing me, but at the same time, it momentarily forced me to look at our family through his eyes.

What did this friend see?

Christa ran the house with seemingly effortless efficiency. She had things down to a science—quickly stripping beds and remaking them with fresh sheets while planning meals in her head like a general drawing up a campaign plan. She presided over conversations at the dinner table with a charm that softened her forcefulness and determination.

WU as the unflappable elder statesman engaged all guests with a courtly manner, observant detachment underneath a veneer of disarming frankness, and sense of humor. With enormous discipline and an ingrained habit of ignoring any physical discomfort, he managed to hide his constant struggle with asthma from nearly everyone except those who knew him well.

Only once, about two years before he died, my father allowed the customary mask of polite reticence slip. We happened to be alone, my mother was away, and I had been delegated to take care of him at my parents' house in Long Island. We watched "The Official Story," a film about the children of the *desaparecido* of Argentina, victims of the forced disappearances that occurred during Argentina's military dictatorship in the 1970s, an era of widespread human rights violations and genocide.

The film depicts the story of an upper-middle-class couple who lives in Buenos Aires with an illegally adopted child. The mother comes to realize that her daughter may be the child of a desaparecido. In one scene, mothers of victims stand on a public square, the Plaza de Mayo in Buenos Aires, and hold up signs and photographs of their children as a form of protest as much in the hope that someone might know more about their fate.

I glanced at my father and realized that he was close to tears. He said it reminded him of the people with signs and photographs at the train stations in Germany at the end of the war, desperate for information about their loved ones. It was a rare instant of remarkable openness evoked by a single raw moment in a film.

But quickly reverting to his customary habit of restraint and understatement, he said that it was a good thing that so much time had passed since then. "*Tempi passati,*" he said, with a curious defeated waving movement of his hands, evoking a world of loss and grief at times gone by.

I was in my early thirties at the time—1989. I had finished graduate school a few years earlier, had a satisfying job as a translator, and had embarked on a research project that fulfilled me. The project was a study of a group of people on the Lower East Side of Manhattan rehabilitating abandoned buildings. As part of my gathering data, I spent a great deal of my free time in the area, interviewing individuals, participating in community events, and even working alongside people doing the labor of rehabilitating their buildings. I loved every minute of it, and the publication of the completed work filled me with pride.

At the same time, I was still spending many weekends in my parents' house and was close to both my parents. One reason that I was willing to admit to myself had to do with the fact that my father was getting older and frailer and that often I was able to help with practical matters around the house. The other reason, harder to acknowledge, was that I found it difficult to detach myself. WU and Christa played a huge role in my life in ways that I loved and hated at the same time, and despite everything that I had done in my adult years, there were times when I felt trapped in measuring my life against that of my parents.

After our many years abroad, my brothers and I felt unmoored from the Germany of the present day, ostensibly our home. At the same time, we did not and could not belong to the world of our parents, especially since much of that was a construct of historical memory and founded on notions of a culture and society that no longer existed. And we felt equally unmoored in America, certainly in the first decades of our lives here. Caught between several worlds, we craved the feeling of belonging somewhere. I envied my parents who inhabited their various worlds of both past and present as if they were walking from one room to the next.

Adrian and I never married. Agostino had married an American with a wonderful, loving family, even though undoubtedly he as well struggled with many of the same doubts as we did. We were averse to commitment and saddled with a confounding mix of a pervasive sense of inadequacy, insecurity, and arrogance, not a good foundation for any relationship. For some of our friends, in particular, those interested in pursuing a relationship with either one of us, our family must have presented a conundrum, alienating and disconcerting.

For years, I chewed over the same questions like a dog with a bone. Would I have had the same courage and moral strength as that displayed by our parents and other family members at various moments in time? Would I have been able to marshal the same sang-froid or the same resilience under pressure? I would never know since I can't walk in someone else's shoes. The need to prove oneself was profound. Ultimately the only thing that might truly satisfy that hunger would be to suffer as much as either of our parents, to demonstrate as much courage, or even to die in battle. Of course, as Adrian joked with me, that scenario would have the disadvantage of depriving us of the enjoyment of our new status as having proven ourselves.

Christa and WU tried to counteract such thoughts by insisting that they simply acted as they had to under challenging circumstances and that one should not compare or measure oneself by the actions of others at other times. However, to understand something rationally doesn't mean one understands it at the level of emotions. Meanwhile, we had internalized the implicit expectation that we had to honor the actions of those who'd come before us in deed or thought. For some of my family members, it led to an almost obsessive-compulsive need to produce as many pieces of writings about our various ancestors as was possible. For others, it led to half-hearted attempts at distancing oneself from the family history.

My brothers and I had become adept at telling stories about our family. When we were at our parents' house, we were like supporting actors in a play, helping Christa to set the scene, or tossing the conversational ball back into her court at the same time as we provided comic relief by our merciless teasing, frequently joined in by my father. Truth and fiction had become blurred, while our own emotions were subsumed by the performance to the point that we did not know them anymore. The act of telling distracted us from our inner doubts as to whether our own lives could ever match up. It was as if we were stuck in a play, waiting for cues from an invisible director.

Overwhelmed by a life we could not lead, my brothers and I in different ways sought refuge in eccentricity and isolation. Living in America helped to liberate us. Here, truly nobody cares about what members of your family may or may not have done—that is, it's interesting, but it doesn't define you as an individual. Meanwhile, my growing confidence also allowed me to return with renewed understanding to the lessons Christa and WU taught us. Like all lessons, these were two-edged swords, containing both emotional traps and profound strengths.

The three of us adopted different stratagems, adjusted as the occasion demanded, in attempting to deal with Christa's habit of friendly takeovers—whether it involved complete separation of worlds, a partial trade pact, or acceptance of her more dominant power. As I got older, it became easier to understand and to be more tolerant of my parents.

Despite my father's increasing frailness, my parents regularly embarked on trips to visit their oldest son in his house in Columbia County and later in Virginia, proud and happy to see their grandsons. In retrospect, I realize how stressful these journeys must have been for my father. As he aged it became increasingly difficult for him to withstand the pressure from his never-ending struggles with asthma. However, Christa and WU traveled as much as was possible. Their last joint trip abroad was in 1996. I accompanied them part of the way, marveling at my parents' cheerful willingness to put up with any discomfort of train travel.

Their final destination in Europe was a villa on a hill in Florence, Italy, the home of Christa's friend from her university days in Prague. I remember watching my father follow Christa up the narrow stone steps to the roof of a *limonaia*, a small stone cottage housing orange and lemon trees in the winter. He barely made it, wheezing and trembling from the effort, but he beamed at Christa with delight. It was a mild October day, and WU, Christa, and their friend sat on top of the limonaia until the sun went down, dipping *biscotti* into *vin santo* and talking about everything under the sun.

MARRIAGE OF TRUE MINDS

Let me not to the marriage of true minds
Admit impediments.
William Shakespeare, Sonnet 116

IN DECEMBER 1998, MY FATHER WAS DIAGNOSED WITH terminal liver cancer.

Typical for Christa, she did not share this with Adrian and me until after Christmas, which we had spent together in Southampton. Her hand was forced in that my father collapsed and was taken to the local hospital by ambulance. At that point, Christa finally revealed to us what she had learned from WU's doctor. The doctor indicated that nothing could be done medically beyond trying to keep him comfortable.

I had been so used to an awareness of my father's frailty and his persistent struggle for breath, combined with an unbending insistence on rejecting all medical aids and medications to make his life easier, that the idea of another serious illness was unreal.

I had moved out to Southampton in 1996, on the heels of completing the research for another book. I wanted to create a life for myself where I could be closer to nature while also becoming part of a local community. Fortunately, I was able to take my job with me. I worked as a translator for a New York City-based company and had already been working from home for some time. The move also made it possible for me to troubleshoot at my parents' house on occasion. Most importantly, the thought of adoption had taken hold of me, and living in a small town with a decent job I could do from home made all this possible.

At the time of my father's diagnosis, I happened to be staying in my parents' house. I had started to renovate my own house, and for several months it was unlivable. For Christa, my presence simplified the decision she had to make as to whether to bring my father back to New York City or to remain in Southampton.

When my father came home from the hospital, we installed him in his bedroom and set up a network of visiting nurses and home care aides. Adrian came frequently from New York City. Agostino's family was in Virginia, and he was not able to visit as often.

Meanwhile, Christa pleaded with us or rather sternly instructed us not to discuss my father's diagnosis with him. To this day I don't understand how the doctor could have told my mother without informing my father. My father was of sound mind.

This created a dilemma for Adrian and me. We both felt that it was wrong to keep my father in the dark. Adrian and I had numerous whispered but no less intense discussions with Christa about withholding the true state of affairs from my father.

Christa froze—that is the only way I could describe it. She insisted that it was better that way. But I suspect that in her fear, desperation, and overwhelming grief, denial was the only way she could manage.

There were several painful house calls from the local doctor in Southampton who had received the same stern instructions from my mother. My father asked the doctor when he would get better and what he could do to help things along. Christa was sitting on a chair next to his bed in line of sight of the doctor, her face a rigid mask. The doctor glanced at her and mumbled something non-committal. I could hardly bear listening.

Meanwhile, one morning when Christa was in another room, my father asked me, "Am I dying? Is this the end for me?"

I happened to be crouching in front of him, trying to adjust the oxygen tank. I looked up and said, "Yes."

"Good girl." My father reached out and patted my arm. "I hope it's going to be fast."

I nodded, barely able to control my emotions.

At that moment, Christa came around the corner into the living room. She looked at me suspiciously, but then let it go.

Looking back on those days, I suspect that she may have at some level welcomed our intervention and appreciated that a burden to tell had been taken from her. WU knew her too well to be surprised by her habit of denial when facing an unbearable situation.

The subsequent weeks were nothing short of miraculous, filled with joy.

We laughed a lot, even while agonizing over the details of the recommended diet for my father. In retrospect, we concluded that we should have just ignored the endless restrictions since the outcome was clear in any event. Instead, dutifully we bought tasteless decaffeinated Earl Grey tea, fed my father bland food, and tried to refrain from giving in to his pleas for salty fried eggs—one of his favorite things to eat. We laughed when my father claimed he was like the Commendatore in *Don Giovanni* as he tried to negotiate the walk from the living room to the bedroom with his walker. "See," he said, lifting the walker and banging it back down onto the tiles. "Boom-boom-boom." We laughed with tears running down

TAPESTRY OF MY MOTHER'S LIFE

our faces when he recited a silly rhyme about a camel being led through the desert by a servant, pointing to the tube leading from his face to the little wheeled oxygen tank, which we had dubbed R2-D2.

And we talked and talked. WU was still reading voraciously. He talked politics with Adrian and helped him to fine-tune a legal brief, wielding his infamous red pen even a few days before he died. He talked with all of us individually about his hopes for us. But what resounds most in my ears is the poetry that filled those days—tossed back and forth between Christa and WU in a continuous dance like the golden ball of life in Münchhausen's poem:

In that wide expanse of the ballroom of time,
I gaze upon the play of life,
Composed and serene,
Everyone passes on the golden ball with a smile,
And none returns the golden ball.

I had read this poem as a child, but it only came alive for me as I watched my parents in those weeks toss lines of verse back and forth to each other as part of an ongoing ceaseless conversation that stretched back into their past and continued until the very end.

Walking into the living room, Christa would hear my father declaim from something he had read, and with a smile she would chime in, picking up where he left off.

"Now, what is that poem about the rider, galloping through the night?" my father asked me one evening. He was in bed, struggling with his oxygen tube and staring up at me in frustration. "I can't remember."

"That's a first." Christa laughed as she stuck her head around the corner and began to recite. "Who rides so swiftly through the night? It was the father with his child. He carries his son in his arms, keeping him safe and keeping him warm."

"Of course, Goethe's "Elf King." How could I not remember that?" WU smiled at us and relaxed on his pillow. He made us get different volumes from all over the house so that he could look up a particular poem. He stuck pieces of paper in between the pages of many collections like helpful markers on the pathways of his thoughts. He hardly needed these markers; he recited these poems, mostly from memory, in between entertaining us with scurrilous rhymes, anecdotes, and balanced commentary on the current state of the world.

There were poems of parting, of gratitude, and of joy.

"Lord, it is time. The summer was great," my father intoned. Christa, walking into the living room with a kitchen towel in her hand, continued, "Lay your shadow now on the sundials, and on the open fields let the winds go!" That was from Rilke's "Autumn Day."

WU loved the wistfulness in Rilke's poem "The Carousel," with the line about festively painted horses, lions, and even elephants going round and round, and coming "from that distant country that hesitates for a long time before it finally sinks beneath the waves." Another favorite was Achim von Arnim's prayer for "wings and a hill of sand; the hill of sand in the beloved fatherland and wings to the soul that's loath to part so that it may fly away from this lovely world with an easy heart." While the familiarity and music of the poem appealed to my father, that particular hill of sand had never mattered to him.

Unlike Christa, WU had not grown up with any comparable attachment to place. While he sympathized with Christa's sense of loss concerning the home of her childhood, his understanding was ultimately an intellectual one without that visceral emotional pull Christa experienced.

The years of unspeakable horrors and devastation wrought at the hand of the Nazis had left my father with indelible emotional scars, shaken in his very foundations by the realization of what his countrymen were capable of.

Everything that he loved in terms of German culture, music, and literature had been touched as if permanently stained by the Nazi regime. Furthermore, he had spent many years abroad before World War II as well as afterward, exacerbating his sense of being a stranger in his own country. My father sought refuge in a kind of inner exile in his pursuit of intellectual pleasures and a stance of detachment. He understood but was not limited by borders, and he carried his country in his soul.

Christa had grown up with an unshakeable sense of roots —roots that reached back over more than half a millennium on her grandfather's land. The Linden tree planted in 1555 in Muttrin served as a flag bearer for Christa's attachment to place. On the other hand, unlike my father, in most respects, Christa had moved on with her life. Perhaps one might instead say she put things behind her, relegating the past to boxes hidden away in a cabinet. The past figured in her conversations only as theatrical props.

The defining force in WU's life was his love for Christa, and ultimately nothing else mattered.

A collection of letters in my basement illustrates this. Filling several book boxes, the letters start in the days when WU and Christa first met and continued throughout their lives. WU wrote almost every day when he was traveling for work, mostly using a fountain pen; Christa used whatever she had at hand.

"Dear Christa, I am so happy I heard your voice on the phone today."

"My dearest, it's been already two days since your last letter."

"Dear *Haschen*, I am so glad you are coming home on Friday."

Haschen was the name they used for each other—a small hare or bunny. Many letters ended with "I miss you."

The letters were lengthy, detailed, pragmatic, and filled

with accounts of everything that happened in their lives. They included descriptions of what my brothers and I were doing, discussions of plans for the summer, and details about house repairs. They expressed concern about matters troubling the other, sent requests on what to purchase and whom to visit, and discussed how to solve problems. They represented an ongoing conversation of two people, with a foundation of trust and love and a willingness to work together at all levels.

Watching my parents in those last weeks, I thought of Shakespeare's sonnet 116, "Let me not to the marriage of true minds admit impediments."

WU knew this sonnet by heart. In the early 1930s, WU and his siblings held a competition with their father, each vying for producing the best translation of this sonnet into German. WU and Christa lived by its central tenet, and it came to full expression once again in those last two months— the laughter, the renewed sense of intimacy Christa treasured in caring for WU, and the shared language of history, culture, and poetry.

An example of the formality and distance in interactions as well as the hidden gulfs of silence was my father's last conversation with his brother, just two days before my father died.

My uncle was never an easy or openly affectionate person; moreover, his relationship with my father was fraught with long-standing conflicts, rooted in their respective relationships with their parents. He had heard from Christa that WU wasn't doing well, and this news inspired him to call from Germany. I happened to watch my father as he answered the phone. He was sitting on his bed, the oxygen tube entangled between his legs, and he was just trying to recover from the exertion of a trip to the bathroom. I could hear only his end of the conversation. Apparently, my uncle asked how he was doing.

"Very well, very well," my father said dismissively, waving his hand as if shooing gnats away. After that, the two brothers immediately embarked on well-trodden paths of familial patterns of communication, laden with unresolved conflicts underneath layers of mutual respect, disdain, and distorted affection. They discussed some books they had been reading and exchanged opinions on the current state of affairs, while carefully refraining from entering old battlefields.

When I had to call my uncle two days later to let him know that his brother had died, he was shocked and appalled that he had so misread my father's offhand comments about his state of health. "I had not expected this," my uncle kept saying.

Toward the end, Christa had made her peace with the inevitable.

"I can't remember the origin of this line," she said to me on the last morning, citing, "And if you do not stake your life, then you will never win life." She added with an expression of chagrin mixed with laughter, "I want to use it for the death notice, but I can't ask him."

In Germany, habitually relatives send out death notices to friends and family as a mirror image of birth announcements, often with a particular bible verse or another quote that is supposed to capture the essence of an individual's life.

That comment made me smile. Of course, even then it was difficult for her to be open with my father about a truth she had a hard time accepting.

"Don't worry, Mima," I told her. "I will ask him."

My father's reaction was typical. "You don't know that? That's pitiful," he said, his eyes twinkling, and launched into a full-throated declamation. "Be of good cheer, comrades, mount your horses and ride forth into battle, toward freedom!"

Christa who walked into the bedroom at that point joined in. "Of course, that's it," she said with evident satisfaction. My father had recited the first lines of a poem called *Reiterlied* by Friedrich von Schiller, which appeared in his three-part drama

Wallenstein. A *Reiterlied* is like a marching song, sung by soldiers on horseback.

It ends in the lines that later appeared in my father's death notice. Three hours later, my father was gone.

WU died at home on March 3, 1999. With grace and composure, Christa made the necessary phone calls and straightened out the room. She placed flowers on the chest of drawers and made sure that a small lamp was turned on throughout the first three nights.

With the same composure, once everything had been done and we had buried my father's ashes, Christa locked the house, got in the car to return to the apartment in New York City, and embarked on the first steps of her new life alone.

❦ 13 ❦

PHOENIX UNCHAINED

THE MEMORIAL SERVICE FOR MY FATHER TOOK PLACE ONE month after his death.

Immediately thereafter, Christa buried herself in work as an art reporter and resumed her social activities. Sometimes the pace with which she pursued her activities verged on the frenetic, almost as if she needed to run away. She traveled back and forth from her apartment in the city to her weekend house in Southampton and on occasion to Germany. She was constantly in a rush.

Sometimes visitors from Europe, whom she liked to drag all over New York City, complained of exhaustion, and she scoffed at them, pleased that she still was more active than anyone around her.

The only time when she was forced to slow down happened in 2000. Christa fell and broke her hip. Immobilized, she cheerfully resigned herself to the temporary state of needing help. It was the only time when she allowed others to take over without any resistance on her part; instead, I can still see her sitting on the porch of her house, wrapped in a blanket, content and at peace, reading Henry James, Jane Austen, and William Makepeace Thackeray.

Meanwhile, in her interactions with others, Christa's ingrained habit of silence and reticence at times contributed to misunderstandings with if not distance from a younger generation in America. In Christa's cultural universe, one didn't talk about one's feelings. One didn't admit to being afraid or unhappy. One didn't say, "I love you," or "I am proud of you." Even anger or frustration generally did not translate into words; it was apparent in a rigid posture, narrowed eyes, and compressed lips—all the more ominous for being contained underneath the surface.

Christa lived her love, her care, and her affection through the stern look that noticed everything, the hand casually adjusting the picture frame since one can't under any circumstances ever have something hang crooked on the wall, and her critical suggestions she volunteered much to our chagrin. Her habitually qualified recognition when we reported an accomplishment was a part of this. Adrian referred to it as being awarded the grade of A-, complaining with frustrated laughter, "Why doesn't she ever give an A?" It was her form of loving us.

Occasionally, I was tempted to act as a "translator" so others would understand her better and not misread her lack of words for a lack of feeling. But I abandoned such attempts; it felt presumptuous to assume others needed such explications and equally presumptuous to assume Christa needed me to defend her.

To my fascination and frustration, I discovered that occasionally Christa communicated more frankly with some of my friends than with me when I was not there. It was as if she needed my absence to relax and show more of her emotions.

When I called from Ukraine in the fall of 2001 to report that I had completed the paperwork for the adoption of my son and had a date for my return flight, she was composed and supportive. She asked what I would need upon arrival at home and how she could help me in the first days. In her typical sensible fashion, she suggested that the convertible crib-junior bed I had purchased before departure be reassembled as a proper bed. I had originally envisioned the adoption of a much younger child. "I will ask Adrian to do that," she said calmly.

Friends who were with her at that time for the Thanksgiving weekend later related her tears and emotions of joy mixed with relief since I had not been able to call for several weeks. When I was present, the ingrained script of reticence ruled our interactions. Perhaps my friends, unencumbered by all the invisible barriers my brothers and I had accepted, found it easier to ask questions, and by the same token for both Christa and WU, the habit of reticence may have been easier to discard with outsiders.

In her last years, Christa became more open with me. However, it didn't occur to me at the time to shed patterns of behavior that dictated listening but not prodding further. Consequently, I missed several opportunities to ask more questions.

The boxes of letters in my basement offer more insights into this same dilemma—openness versus silence, cryptic references versus expansive descriptions. Like storytelling, letters served as a medium for keeping silent, a form of concealment underneath a voluble and expressive speech.

Spending time with my son was a joy and a distraction for Christa, a new part of her life that she embraced with enthusiasm. The geographic proximity between my home and hers made this easy. Sadly, my brother's sons lived in Virginia, and interactions were limited to the annual visit during the summer.

Meanwhile, in 2003 Christa received a diagnosis of multiple myeloma. This type of cancer can be managed if not cured for a while before progressing to the final stage. We learned of this only in the form of veiled hints about the possibility that there might be something wrong with some tests her doctor had been running. It took a while to get a more complete picture. Over the next six years, my mother lived through every form of chemo imaginable as well as repeated radiation treatments.

During the first years after Christa's diagnosis, it seemed inconceivable that anything would change. Even though Adrian and I pored over the literature of her form of cancer and discussed the side effects of various treatment options, we could not reconcile the reality of the diagnosis with her life, watching her continue business as usual with her customary energy and determination.

Christa's modus operandi throughout was denial. Sickness was something that happened to other people. She continued going to auctions and writing about the art market and maintained an active social life. She even accompanied my son and me on several short field trips such as Mystic Seaport and Tanglewood, never complaining about exhaustion and intent on ensuring that my son had a good time.

By about 2005, the cancer was progressing and eroding Christa's ability to pretend that nothing was wrong. However, it did not affect her stubborn and relentless determination to remain in complete control at all times.

Adrian, who did not have the benefit of a family to shelter behind, became the point man in New York City, helping Christa with her computer, her phone, and technology in general, as well as accompanying her to the hospital for treatments and making sure she got home safely afterward. While she was in Southampton, my son and I stayed with her at her house, so that she would not be alone.

My son was more perceptive about how much pain Christa experienced than I was. Whenever she arrived in Southampton for the weekend, we picked her up at the bus station. At home, my son would run to get her pain medicine before she even asked for it. He also brought a spoon and a jam jar, since he knew that she found it easier to eat pills with a little bit of jam. He would stand in front of her, watching her intently until she had swallowed.

I had several acrimonious discussions with Christa over her unwillingness to accept more help in her apartment. One of these discussions landed me in the penalty box for several months after I had suggested that Adrian could not be there for her all the time. Another involved her precarious driving habits and my attempts to intervene; she refused to talk to me for weeks.

Adrian with whom I spoke almost every day sometimes left messages on my phone, expressing his frustration.

"I am going to have to shoot our mother or myself," he said one day when describing the scene outside the hospital after hours of treatment. Christa, true to form, wanted to take the bus and refused the taxi Adrian was willing to pay for as an unnecessary expense. A wheelchair was acceptable as long as Christa was inside the confines of the hospital; once on the street she shook off Adrian's arm, leaning against the wall in her weakness, but upright.

And yet, there were many wonderful times; for instance, for my son's birthday celebration she took Adrian, my son, and me to see a performance of Don Giovanni at the Metropolitan Opera. Another time, she came with us to help choose a dog from the shelter and bring him home, delighted to have another being she could spoil. In 2007, I had to move out of the house in which I had been living with my son. Christa immediately suggested that we stay in her house until I had found another solution. In this emergency as well as in countless others, Christa was a rock, calm, sensible, and supportive.

I remember the last year of Christa's life as a blur. As she got sicker and was less able to withstand the effects of treatment, she increasingly suffered from moments of utter confusion. At the same time, she was as ever steadfast in refusing to admit how sick she was or to allow us to help her.

The beginning of the end came with the death of her cousin Lothar. Strictly speaking, he had been a cousin only by marriage to Christa's first husband. He had been like an older brother to us and lived in my parents' house in Long Island for many months each year. Christa loved him, and he represented part of her youth and her first marriage.

As it happened, he died of a heart attack in Christa's house while she was in her apartment in New York City. My son and I had gone out for pizza on the first day of the school year; when we returned to my mother's house, it was already too late. Perhaps if I had walked into the house a few minutes earlier I might have been able to get Lothar help in time. Adrian, whom I called in desperation after the ambulance had come and gone, took on the task of telling Christa about this by going to her apartment in the morning.

Meanwhile, even though struggling with her grief, Christa went out of her way to reassure me. "I knew he had heart problems. He told me, and he chose not to do anything about it."

I did not entirely believe her, but I was beyond grateful for her saying this. I knew how close she and Lothar had always been.

Despite exhaustion and nausea from chemo treatments, Christa continued to insist on doing things her way. Thus, in December 2008, she placed a carp, smoked duck, and a Christmas pudding in her bag and traveled on the bus to Southampton where she struggled with the preparations for the holidays. This was as amusing as it was infuriating.

Two months later, in February 2009, Adrian was diagnosed with cancer. The prognosis was grim despite the option of a transplant. Again, Christa was calm when confronted with this news. The only time she came close to breaking down was after Adrian had undergone treatment in preparation for the transplant. She had visited him in the hospital, unprepared for the impact of extensive chemotherapy on his appearance. When she called me, she was in tears. "I didn't recognize him," she told me. "How could I not recognize him?"

Aside from that brief moment of raw emotion, Christa was steady and composed even while her health was steadily deteriorating. On the day Adrian died, for the first and only time in my life, Christa was willing to listen to me and did exactly what I asked her to do. That is, I had to call her from my house in Long Island to let her know that Adrian had had a heart attack and that I was on my way to the city. I had to chase her down in the hospital across the street from the one where Adrian was. She had gone in for treatment and had planned to visit Adrian after she was done. I dreaded the thought of her having to go into the intensive care unit.

"Is it the end?" she asked in a quiet voice when the nurse at her hospital finally handed her the phone.

"Yes, I believe so." I tried to match her tone. She hardly needed to hear my sense of desperation. I was Adrian's healthcare proxy and had just given the hospital permission to refrain from resuscitating him if he should have another heart attack as they expected.

"What would you like me to do?"

"Go home."

"I will," she said. "I will wait for you at home."

This helped steady me as I made arrangements to travel into the city. When I finally reached Christa's apartment, she was at the door.

"I made tea." And then, again typical for Christa, she was thinking beyond herself. "This is so hard for you," she said.

We sat in the living room and drank tea, quietly and calmly, in complete understanding.

No mother should have to live to see her child die. If I could have reversed the order, I would gladly have spared Christa this time. And yet, selfishly I was beyond grateful to be able to be with her after Adrian's death. There was nobody else who understood as well and who knew how close we had been.

In the following days, I went back and forth from Long Island to New York City, dealing with Adrian's affairs and trying to clean out his rental apartment as quickly as possible. I felt it was urgent to do so. I suspected my mother's time was running out, and I wanted to be able to focus on her. However, everything moved faster than I had anticipated.

For a few weeks, Christa was clear and composed. She tried to help me figure out what to do with Adrian's possessions. There was one moment where I almost burst out laughing. I told her that I planned to pass certain objects of Adrian's on to various friends of his. Christa fixed her eagle eye on me, frowning in concentration, and then said, "I will have to think about that," evidently not fully approving my decisions. Here she was, on her way out the door, and yet still firmly determined to control everything as she saw fit. Adrian would have loved it.

Meanwhile, on the day the movers came to remove the last bits of furniture from Adrian's apartment, Christa had reached the end of her rope, dissolving into a state of complete confusion and physical collapse. Agostino brought her to Sloan Kettering. There, she was treated for a few days. But eventually, her doctor, who had cared for her during the last six years, washed his hands like Pontius Pilate and stepped away from all involvement. He told Agostino that she had to be taken to a hospice facility in the Bronx.

I don't blame this doctor for his decision; however, I blame him for how he handled this moment. There was no bridge between years of friendship-like conversations between the doctor and Christa and that moment when he decided he could no longer treat her, stepped out of the room, and said "Get her out of here."

Christa meanwhile, somewhat revived after having been given copious liquids, insisted on attending Adrian's memorial service in Long Island. With the support of a nurse willing to come along for the ride, Agostino managed to bring Christa out to Southampton, where I hoped to be able to manage things with the help of home care and hospice workers.

That night Christa was so ill that I was convinced she wouldn't make it until the next morning. But once again, I was wrong, underestimating her willpower. I reached a state of almost hysterical frustration and laughter when she refused to be taken into the church in a wheelchair. Instead, supported, or more properly dragged, by Agostino and a friend of ours, she made her way down the aisle to the front row. Sitting next to her on the wooden bench, with my arm wrapped around her skinny frame, I thought *she is attending her own service.*

After the service, we returned to Christa's house, where Agostino had prepared food for all the guests. That afternoon demonstrated once again the extent to which Christa had been successful in creating resilient webs linking our various worlds. The friends who attended were as much Christa's friends as Adrian's and had all spent a great deal of time with us during weekends at the house on Long Island or in the apartment in New York City. Christa held court. Presiding in her chair on the porch, she talked to everyone, while guarded by my son who insisted on fixing the straw in her drinking glass, cutting her food, and making sure she ate something.

The next day, everybody left, and the agony started. Her cancer had taken over, and in her confusion and pain, overwhelmed by grief, desperation, and fear, Christa reverted to her time-honored survival instincts that centered on never ceding control and never giving up. She wanted to return to New York City at all cost—never mind that she couldn't stand up by herself anymore, was already receiving morphine, and had the hospice nurse checking in regularly.

Christa fought us all, the hospice nurse, the home care aide, and me, and we were helpless against her rage. The only exception was my son, who succeeded in giving her medicine when nobody else could do it. At one point, after struggling with the home care aide, Christa tried to call the police. The hospice people and the homecare aide were ready to throw in the towel and wanted to leave, recommending that Christa be taken to the nearby hospice facility.

Finally, when I had to be away from the house, she managed to lock herself in the bathroom. The home care aide called me, asking me to return as quickly as I could.

How can I get through the next months? I kept thinking as I drove back. *I can't even manage a single day taking care of her.* Despite all evidence to the contrary and despite having signed the paperwork with the hospice workers, I hadn't taken in the reality that the end was near. Faced with Christa's habitual willpower and resilience, all I could think of was my fear of not being able to manage her care while hanging on to my job and taking care of my son.

Adrian and I had frequently talked about this sort of scenario, both of us frustrated to no end by the steadily deteriorating situation of Christa's existence in her apartment. We tried everything we could think of to arrange for regular help. Christa blocked it all. Adrian at one point threw up his hands and said, "Shit is going to happen. There is nothing we can do."

Of course, he didn't envision this final scenario of our mother locking herself into her bathroom. I had to break the lock to get inside. Christa sat there, cowering on the toilet, frozen into resistance. To my everlasting regret and grief, in my despair, I could not think of anything better to do than to kneel in front of her, look her in the eyes, and say, "Mima, where do you want to die? Here at home or in the hospital?"

It was as if the fight went out of her at that moment. She allowed me to help her up and take her back to her bed. A day later, she stopped talking altogether.

Christa died exactly one week after the memorial service for her son.

My initial feeling was that of overwhelming relief. The fight was over. I wouldn't have to face yet another situation over the coming weeks where I would fail my mother by being unable to take care of her properly. In the morning she had been in pain, and in my panic and wish to make the pain go away, I almost broke the little bottle of morphine that the hospice nurse had placed into the refrigerator. My hand shook when I finally put some drops in my mother's mouth. I was glad that in the end, she had just quietly passed away.

In the first few hours after Christa's death, after taking the homecare aid to the train station and calling Agostino and the funeral home, I was content to be alone in the house. I did the same things my mother had done after my father's death—making the room neat, arranging flowers, and turning on a light on the nightstand. When everything was done and the kind man from the funeral home had come and gone, I went around the house closing up before returning to my own house where friends had been taking care of my son.

Two days later, when I returned to Christa's house, I was stunned to find all the doors wide open. The summer breeze blew in from the porch, moving the curtains.

Of course, in my rational mind, I realize that it is entirely likely that in my exhaustion I simply forgot to close the doors. And yet, the sight filled me with elation. Christa had escaped after all. She was not to be managed nor controlled. She had found a way out.

When I was going through the books on Christa's nightstand, the ones that she had always kept with her, I came across a small, musty-smelling one entitled *Hasenroman*, or *The Romance of the Rabbit* by Francis Jammes, with a dedication from WU, "To my dearest little bunny, a romance of a bunny."

The last scene describes the rabbit's death, characterized by a stubborn, unrelenting refusal to give in until the very end, in words like a love song to what life had been.

"His heartbeat grew weaker and weaker; this heart which used to flutter like the pale wild rose in the wind dissolving at the morning hour when the hedge softly caresses the lambs. ... Suddenly his hair stood erect, and he became like unto the stubble of summer where he formerly dwelled beside his sister, the quail, and the poppy, his brother; and like unto the clayey earth which had wetted his beggar's paws; and like unto the gray-brown color with which September days clothe the hill whose shape he had assumed; like unto the rough cloth of Francis; like unto the wagon-track on the roadway from which he heard the packs of hounds with hanging ears, singing like the angelus; like unto the barren rock which the wild thyme loves. In his look, where now floated a mist of bluish night, there was something unto the blessed meadow where the heart of his beloved awaited him at the heart of the wild sorrel. The tears which he shed were like unto the fountain of the seraphs at which sat the old fisher of eels repairing his lines. He was like unto life, like unto death, like unto himself, like unto Paradise." (Jammes, 1920, p. 20).

GROOMING GHOSTS

I seem to move in a world of ghosts,
And feel myself the shadow of a dream.
Alfred Lord Tennyson, "The Princess"

IF I HAD READ TENNYSON AS A CHILD, I MIGHT HAVE identified with the princess of the poem bearing the same name.

My family had a plethora of ghosts.

Of course, there was the obligatory assortment of standard ghosts—the ones that behave in an orderly fashion, well-regulated and predictable. Most of these came from my mother's side of the family.

Christa remembered visiting her paternal grandmother as a child. She would sit in her grandmother's boudoir and listen to stories about ghosts that appeared in the Studnitz house where my grandfather was born.

Some stories involved mysterious cracks in the wall of the castle that appeared three days before a member of the family died. Over the years, there must have been a lot of cracks, since so many members of the family lost their lives in various wars.

Other stories had to do with the presumed existence of water veins underneath the house. There is no scientific evidence substantiating any such notions, prevalent in many German tales. Yet, to this day one can find people who are ready to attribute all sorts of events, health issues, and disturbances to the existence of underground water currents. In Christa's stories, whenever something impeded the course of these water veins the house would be restless and disaster would strike.

Appropriate in a house haunted by ghosts, the existence of a piano that played by itself goes without saying as do steps in the night and servants afraid to stay in the house. And, of course, all portents of horrible things to befall the family came in threes. Again, this also was just as it should be.

These ghosts never bothered me. Their range of action was confined to specific spaces and circumstances. There was something reassuring about them—pleasantly spooky, familiar, and predictable as a Grimm's fairytale.

I loved them as much as I loved Zickelbart whose intermittent appearance in my mother's stories about her childhood was ultimately that of a benevolent if infinitely sad spirit. He was one of many frayed threads in a rich and colorful tapestry woven by her voice. That Zickelbart was just a fragment did not matter to us. The mere mention of this name evoked a lost and endlessly charming world conveyed to us through Christa's images.

No, the ghosts that haunted my brothers and me throughout our lives were of a different caliber. We contended with corporal ghosts as much as with disembodied ones. They shaped us and left indelible imprints on our emotions. The corporal ghosts came in the form of various objects we grew up with, pieces of furniture, and entire houses. Then there were the ghosts of the departed, ghostly family secrets and shadows of the unknown, recurring ghostly temper tantrums, and waking nightmares.

An entire house became one of the most prominent and formidable ghosts for my brothers and me. It was my paternal grandmother's house outside of Munich, an eclectic mix of a Swiss-style chalet combined with a French manor at the edge of a picturesque Bavarian village. The huge, neglected garden featured a long-abandoned swimming pool, filled with leaves and trees sprouting from the bottom. We visited there often, sometimes staying for several weeks at a time during school holidays. My grandmother shared the house with her oldest daughter, her sister, her sister's companion, and the cook—five elderly ladies, all dressed in black, with silvery hair chastely wound around their heads and secure with long pins.

It fit the job description of a creepy house, starting with a dark hallway with a loudly ticking grandfather clock and a mysterious room incomprehensibly filled with rows of sewing machines. As a child peeking inside that room, I envisioned invisible people sitting at those tables with the sewing machines humming.

Years later, I learned that in the first years after the war, refugees, who lived in the house, worked in this room in a form of *Heimarbeit*—work from home instead of going to a workshop or factory. For reasons that escape me no one bothered to remove the sewing machines once the refugees had found housing.

My father's contribution to this half-imagined world was his reference to "Oblomov on the couch." For years, I was convinced that we had an odd relative called Oblomov who spent much of his time sleeping. I became rather fond of Oblomov, largely because my father spoke of him with such amused affection. In fact, it happened to be a hapless refugee of Russian extraction who resided there for a time, christened by my father after a character in a novel by the Russian writer Ivan Goncharov. Ilya Ilyich Oblomov is a young nobleman who rarely leaves his room or bed.

Each bedroom on the second floor was equipped with a

sink with chipped enamel, threadbare curtains, and a cast-iron stove with an old copper kettle that had not been used in years. We slept on twin beds with lumpy mattresses and comforters that bunched up like inflated sacks of flour and were too short to cover one's feet.

Dark mahogany furniture lined the walls of the long hallway. In an alcove, hobbyhorses and walking sticks with snakeheads crowded together in umbrella stands, shape-shifting in the half-light of the afternoon. The bathroom held no terrors, only old-fashioned and reassuring discomfort—a hot-water boiler on the wall, a rusty tub, never used, drawers full of empty bottles, saved by my grandmother in case of another war, enameled pitchers used for carrying hot water to the bedrooms, and a wicker basket filled with shoe polish and brushes.

The attic contained my grandaunt's dowry chests, piles of etchings of battleships, Charlemagne, and the Virgin Mary, dusty riding boots hanging from the ceiling, and sewing models—like headless actors lost in the back wings of a theater.

The room at the end of this hallway was round; from the outside, that part of the house looked like Rapunzel's tower, the ivy doubling for her long braid. Crowded bookshelves underneath the bay windows, faded Persian carpets, and a black stove formed a perfect setting for ghostly characters out of old stories—invariably cursing the owner of a castle and dying on the same spot, always to reappear at the stroke of midnight as a bundle of groaning, stinking, creaking rags that spoke in a scratchy voice.

Meanwhile, all these features pale in significance when set against the pedestals in honor of my grandfather all over the house. These pedestals came in the form of closets full of documents and writings we were allowed to peek at before they were removed from our untutored eyes, and a marble bust and as well as a marble relief featuring my grandfather.

My grandmother lost no opportunity to remind us of the nature of his death at the hand of the Nazis, with a morbid form of sadistic pleasure spelling out the gory details to me repeatedly when I was a child.

My grandmother was not the only one to indulge in this sort of thing. My grandaunt, who lived in the same house, took us for afternoon walks, invariably leading us onto a big field with an old oak tree in the middle. My grandaunt never failed to point out that two children had sought refuge underneath that same tree during a storm only to be struck and killed by lightning.

At the time, I did not question our aunt's notion of entertainment on our afternoon walk or my grandmother's gruesome retelling of my grandfather's death. My brothers and I were habituated to it, observing it almost as a form of theater performance for our benefit. However, my grandmother's story became the cornerstone of an entire edifice that haunted me and still haunts me to this day. And yet, perversely it also fills me with longing for the days when I sat on my little stool in my grandmother's room and listened to her animated voice, enthralled by her charm, and indulging in fantasies of rewriting the story and altering the ending.

My father, in a remarkably forgiving attempt to excuse his mother's behavior, said that perhaps this was the only way she could manage her feelings.

As an adult, I learned to appreciate more and more that my father was keenly aware of the danger of burdening us with these ghosts of the past. He was for himself unable to detach himself from the tentacle-like hooks that kept pulling him back over and over. Yet, he welcomed and encouraged our attempts to move beyond it into a new world. Sadly, my father's reluctance in imposing the past on us never provided a sufficient counterweight for my grandmother's utter lack of restraint on this point. He left a vacuum into which her relentless and brutal insistence could flow like floodwaters during a storm.

Our days in our grandmother's house were dominated by stories about our grandfather, marked by an absence of personal details about him as a real, living, breathing human being rather than just an awe-inspiring figure on a pedestal, and by stories about the lost boys.

The lost boys were the sons of my father's sister Fey, who together with other so-called kin prisoners of members of the resistance had been interned until the end of the war.

The two children, ages four and eighteen months at the time, had been removed by the Gestapo on the day of my aunt's arrest. While my aunt was eventually released at the end of World War II, the whereabouts of her sons were unknown. Fey was reunited with her husband in Italy in May 1945, however, was not able to obtain a travel permit to go to Germany to search for her sons. They were found by my grandmother in the course of an arduous search through war-torn Germany, traveling from orphanage to orphanage wherever children of members of the resistance of Hitler were thought to be. In July 1945, she arrived at an orphanage in Austria, where she was told that they had two boys that fit the description. The two boys had been given new last names and were about to be released for adoption when my grandmother arrived at the orphanage. Fortunately, the older one immediately recognized her. The younger one was confused. However, once she showed him photographs of his home, he recalled the name of a family pet. Thus, the orphanage accepted the identification and released the boys into my grandmother's custody. The boys had been apart from their mother for thirteen months.

The story of their abduction and ultimate rescue was told to us over and over again when we were children. With sickened fascination, I imagined the scene of the older boy screaming as one of the women working for the Gestapo carried him away. We relived the loss of the children so many times that despite the story's invariably triumphant conclusion they always remained lost in my imagination.

Our cousins grew up in Italy and spent much of their lives there. The scar tissue they had received as a result of their experiences at a very young age shaped and defined them in ways beyond their control. One distinguished himself by being detached and cool in his interpersonal relations. The other, in the description of another cousin, was a permanently restlessly searching soul, hiding his fragile self under a mask of laughter and intensity, reminiscent of the sad clown Pagliaccio from Leoncavallo's opera Il Pagliacci, whose performance blurred the lines between what was truth and what was fiction.

They were fascinating older cousins whom we met during our annual visits to Italy while my family still lived in Europe. Despite a complete familiarity, in part due to their strong family resemblance and mannerisms that we recognized and enjoyed, that distance was never bridged. The lost boys were more real in my imagination than these delightful strangers who made us laugh with their grace, expressive features, and vivid gestures. I loved these cousins, and yet I never was able to look at them as individuals, but instead was locked into seeing them as the lost boys.

Undoubtedly it is odd to think of a piece of furniture as a ghost. We had several.

To provide a context for this, most pieces of furniture in my family came with history hard to shake off. This could be their age, having been in the family's possession for hundreds of years, or their secret compartments, revealing intriguing bundles of unexpected correspondence, or scars of violence such as the marks of the boot of the Gestapo officer who kicked my grandfather's writing desk when arresting my grandfather in his office in the summer of 1944.

One piece of furniture, in particular, haunted me throughout my childhood although I never even saw it. It was my maternal grandfather's writing desk. There is no photo-graph of it, but I imagined it looked like my father's, that is, made of burl walnut with an inset green leather top, and drawers on both sides. Meanwhile, that's irrelevant.

"It was lost when the Wall was built," my mother told me when I was a child. "We were never able to get it out."

"The desk behind the Wall" acquired a life of its own in my imagination. I linked this perplexing information to my vague grasp of the historical event involving the construction of the Berlin Wall. For years, I imagined the desk in a room in an apartment in the center of Berlin, standing at a slant to catch some of the light from the window, perhaps with a silver inkwell and an embossed leather folder on its surface. I pictured soldiers appearing in the middle of the night to build a wall, cutting the apartment in two.

I considered this scenario entirely plausible since I had grown up with the story my father liked to tell us—the tale of two brothers of an Italian family, distantly related by marriage to my father's sister. The brothers shared a palazzo in Florence. However, they argued with each other, and finally, one brother took matters into his hands and constructed a wall through the middle of the palazzo.

Thus, sometimes in my dreams, I saw my grandfather's desk standing all by itself and forgotten in an empty room, with one corner poking through the concrete wall. I worried about the desk, but I never questioned the story. In later years, I forgot to ask my mother.

Meanwhile, the closing of the border between East and West Berlin occurred during the night, beginning at midnight on August 13, 1961. The construction of the concrete wall took over a year, and the government of the GDR continued working on it until the early 1980s.

My maternal grandmother, who lived in the Soviet Occu-pation zone at the end of World War II, managed to bring some of her possessions to the West in 1951. However, the desk had to be left behind.

The first time I heard the lyrics of Leonard Cohen's song "Who by Fire," I immediately thought of my family. Cohen's lyrics were based on the Jewish prayer for atonement on Yom Kippur, *Unetaneh tokef.*

> *Who shall perish by water and who by fire,*
> *Who by sword and who by wild beast,*
> *Who by famine and who by thirst,*
> *Who by earthquake and who by plague,*
> *Who by strangulation and who by stoning,*
> *Who shall have rest and who shall wander,*
> *Who shall be at peace and who shall be pursued,*
> *Who shall be at rest and who shall be tormented,*
> *Who shall be exalted and who shall be brought low,*
> *Who shall become rich and who shall be impoverished?*

Over and over, I repeated the list in my mind. It fit my family—drowned, blown up, hanged, by powder, by poison, by starvation, by slow decay, by war, and by silence.

Some of our ancestral ghosts were funny to us when we were children. One was an aunt by marriage who lived on what at one point in time had been a small, landed estate. According to the story told in the family, one day, after having imbibed copious amounts of "sweet wine," she drowned in a shallow stream running through the property. This body of water was known as the *Schweinegraben*, i.e., the pig ditch.

Another ancestor, Henriette Vogel, my three-times-great-grandmother, joined the poet Heinrich von Kleist in a suicide pact. I was fascinated by her story, yet terrified and mystified at the same time. With youthful callous and judgmental ignorance of what lay behind our ancestress' act as well as devoid of patience with the fervor of the Romantic Age, I considered her choice in seeking out Kleist's support as melodramatic and incomprehensible. Other family members referred to her dismissively as *cuckoo*, placing the index finger suggestively on the temple.

Only later I learned the tragic story behind this; Henriette Vogel suffered from an untreatable form of uterine cancer. She decided that death was preferable to the likely scenario of a painful end. Meanwhile, she feared taking such a step by herself. Aware of Kleist's suicidal thoughts and having already developed a close friendship with him based on their love of music and literature, she asked him to join forces with her. On November 21, 1811, after penning letters to their respective families, Kleist first shot Henriette Vogel and then himself on the bank of Kleiner Wannsee, a lake in Berlin.

Do I count my great-grandfather among these ghosts?

Alfred von Tirpitz was a looming figure, imposing by virtue of his forked, snow-white beard, his massive size, and his role in German history as Grand Admiral and Secretary of State of the German Imperial Naval Office from 1897 until 1916. When my brothers and I were adults, we would burst into horrified laughter when coming across yet another of the seemingly endless atrocious portraits that displayed his beard and piercing eyes to the point of caricature, often showing him with a lethal-looking trident in his hand in a not-so-subtle reference to Poseidon, the god of the sea.

However, Tirpitz's image was softened for us by the endearing stories told by my father, including his love of his grandchildren, indulging them by playing with them in the red currant bushes where the children would compete in tossing red berries at his beard and his enjoyment of his grandchildren's books.

My father used to show us how Tirpitz would assess the atmospheric pressure by knocking with his index finger against a barometer. This same barometer hung in my parents' house, and I sometimes secretly knocked against it, trying to recreate the picture of my great-grandfather testing the world before taking action.

Another ghostly impression was the experience of listening to my grandfather Hassell in a video clip showing the trial in the court presided over by Roland Freisler. It was disconcerting to hear a voice of someone whom I never met in person and yet whose voice was familiar to me in its intonation and even its pitch—relatively high just like my father's brother's voice—disembodied tendrils reaching through time and space.

Then, of course, there were the relatives who disappeared from view. In the version of the family history penned by my Hassell great-grandfather, there appears the phrase about a male member of the family, "He gave my father so much grief that I will say no more about him here." Several died under suspicious circumstances, with a veil of silence over what exactly happened. Others are mentioned only with the cryptic comment that, due to their unspecified misdeeds, they were sent to America, never to be heard from again. Adrian worked hard at trying to find out what happened to these individuals, but to our disappointment, the trail had run cold.

One of my granduncles was referred to only in dismissive tones as someone who was deemed defective. As a child, I lived under the impression that he was institutionalized and at a very minimum severely mentally disabled. Only years later, I learned from another relative that this granduncle had served in the military and had achieved the rank of lieutenant colonel.

The relative told me that as far as he knew, my granduncle had suffered from a lack of oxygen at birth, which presumably resulted in long-term disabilities and developmental delays, and he described him as a kind, quiet, and dignified man. He was essentially written out of the historical record. It reflects a brutal and callous dismissal of those not considered "heroic" or "up to the standards" imagined for the family, a dismissal perpetrated by my Hassell grandmother and to a lesser degree by her children, who acquiesced in this silence.

On Christa's side of the family, there exists a long list of men who died in World War I and another long list of those who lost their lives in World War II. This includes my grandfather, my mother's brother, four of five cousins, and the father of these cousins.

My maternal grandmother's sister and her husband took their own lives during the last days of World War II, swept up in a wave of utter exhaustion and despair that had gripped many residents of a region about to be overrun by the Soviet army. I learned of this only in fragments over the years. It haunted me, and the weight of their choice was multiplied by the silence of my grandmother and mother as well as other family members on this subject.

Other lost ghosts include the Jewish members of my family. Again, we learned of this only when we were already grown up, literally stumbling over the information that our Hassell grandmother's grandfather Gustav Lipke had been baptized at age eighteen to facilitate his entering public service. We managed to piece together more details about Lipke's ancestors, largely thanks to the work of Adrian. He managed to trace these relatives as far back as the 18th century to Moses Simion, a rabbi born 1750 in Königsberg (Kaliningrad), who later became a teacher in Berlin. Meanwhile, he was not able to make the same connections from our 19th century ancestors forward other than our own family. The specter of the probable fate of some of these distant relatives at the hands of the Nazis cannot be dismissed. In my grandmother's family, the veil of silence was complete, presumably to protect her and her siblings.

Of course, many of these fates were hardly unusual for their time and place. And the impenetrable blanket of silence is also found over and over again. I suppose in our case it was not only that we had to contend with the sheer volume of these stories and the thick fog surrounding them; it was their juxtaposition with the ghosts of another caliber, heroes writ large whom one could not evade as a member of the family.

In addition to all the ghosts not talked about, there were photographs of two men on my father's writing desk. The frames had become brittle, and the photographs faded and yellow, but they remained in their usual spot behind the inkwell. My father never explained. Christa told us that these were friends who died in World War II, while my father lay ill, close to death, in a hospital in Switzerland. Throughout his life after the war, my father carried the scars of someone who survived, having lost many of his friends and peers in addition to his father. He did not talk about them, and nor did he ever talk directly about what it was like to lose his father under such horrific circumstances.

Finally, there are the ghosts of our dreams.

An odd feature of my genetic makeup is a pattern of waking nightmares inherited from my father, who in turn inherited this from his father.

The stories I heard about my grandfather in this context are hilarious. Ulrich von Hassell, whom I can never imagine as younger than the dignified age of sixty-three he had reached at the time of his execution, all his life was plagued by nightmares. Oftentimes, these forced him out of his bed in the middle of the night desperate to escape from some imagined terror. Repeatedly my grandmother would find him cowering under a table, shivering in his pajamas, and convinced that he was in a cave with icicles dribbling onto his neck. The icicles turned out to be the water drops from a flower vase he had knocked over.

Another nightmare became part of family lore. While stationed as General Counsel in Barcelona in the 1920s, my grandfather acquired a painting in a junk shop for the proud sum of 120 Pesetas, in 2021 roughly 280 dollars. Attributed to a 15th-century Flemish painter from the school of Rogier van der Weyden, the painting depicts a Madonna, with her elongated hands held in prayer and her head gently inclined to the side. It accompanied him throughout all his diplomatic posts.

In 1926, my grandfather was posted to Copenhagen where he served as general counsel. According to the story related by my grandmother, one night he suffered from a nightmare. He woke up, with the echo of several dull thuds ringing in his ears. After a few moments of collecting himself, he rushed downstairs, spurred by an instinct that something was wrong. A fire had broken out in the drawing-room. While shouting for his wife and the servants, he proceeded to dump buckets of water onto the flames and to rip the curtains off the windows. Eventually, he and the rest of the household managed to put out the fire. It had done considerable damage to the furnishings and numerous oil paintings.

Meanwhile, the Madonna was unharmed. However, mysteriously, the painting had detached itself from its hook and catapulted first onto the fireplace mantle and from there onto the floor. These had been the dull thuds my grandfather had heard in his dream. Thereafter, my grandmother always insisted that the Madonna had protected them in gratitude for her rescue from the flea market.

My grandmother enjoyed telling us this story, embellishing it with enthusiasm, and in her retelling, the Madonna began to acquire mythical proportions. As a child, one of my favorite things was to stop in front of her, suspended above a chest of drawers with dark wood and a vase of fresh flowers underneath. I liked to gaze at her gentle face and the elongated fingers, imagining their soft touch.

My father also suffered from these nightmares; they inspired him to lash out while he was not yet fully awake, knocking over furniture and lamps in the process and at times hitting my mother in the dark before she managed to stop him. She usually laughed about it in the morning.

My nightmares follow a similar pattern. In the minutes

between waking up in the clutch of sheer terror and finally realizing that it was just a dream, I have knocked over lamps, turned on the light in my son's room, accosted him with nonsensical questions, or even written out my last wishes because it seemed of the utmost urgency that I do so right then. My son learned to react pragmatically and calmly to these scenes.

Meanwhile, the crowning glory of such amblings in the dark of night occurred three days after my maternal grandmother's death, on a day that happened to coincide with her birthday on April 1.

Now, to provide a context for this, my grandmother's fierce and volatile temper had not abated in her old age. Her temper was such that hired nurses were afraid of her even when she was well over ninety. Christa was not the only one who feared this; we all took care to tread lightly around her, fearing the explosions. It was as if a ghost or dybbuk walked with her through all the years of her life. We were treated to a final visitation shortly after her death.

When my grandmother died in her apartment in Bonn, my mother traveled ahead of us. Adrian and I came two days later, arriving from New York on the evening of the third day after my grandmother's death. Overtired and yet restless, we joined my mother in her efforts to straighten out the apartment for the guests, due to arrive on the day of the memorial service. My grandmother had never allowed anyone of us to do anything remotely like that. She would have considered such actions outrageous interference in her life. Hence, our cleaning, sorting, and poking in corners felt akin to grave robbing.

Finally, my mother insisted that we go to bed. I was assigned the couch in the dining room. My mother stayed in the guestroom, and my brother, undismayed by the notion of ghosts, retreated to my grandmother's bedroom. Exhausted, we fell asleep.

The next thing I knew was that I needed to escape as quickly as I could. Banging against unfamiliar walls, pushing obstacles out of the way, I thundered my way through the dark until finally, a light came on.

"Did the war break out?" Adrian stood in the living room, blinking at me, his hair tousled.

I was out of breath, bruised, and with my hands cut, still in the grip of overwhelming panic. At this point my mother appeared from her bedroom, looking small and frail in her nightgown.

Wordlessly we stared at the disaster. I had knocked over a large glass cabinet filled with heavy vases, gold-edged mocha cups, and other fine china so that it tilted and hit the dining room table. I had pushed it further along the table where it left scars that exist to this day, made my way around the corner, ripped a wooden Madonna off the wall, and pushed a bookshelf out of the way, knocking the collected works of Schiller and Goethe and other luminaries of classical German literature onto the floor.

Remarkably, the glass doors of the cabinet had not broken. The contents of the cabinet were another matter. The heavy vases on the bottom shelves had contributed to the racket by rolling back and forth on the cabinet's journey along the table edge. Ironically, most of these truly atrociously ugly vases survived. Adrian later said that at first in his tired confusion he had decided someone was shifting bags of coal on the roof. Regrettably, it took him a while to wake up completely and to realize that something else was happening.

After a long silence, my mother began to laugh. "This was Nuna's last temper tantrum," she said finally. It was April 1, the day of my grandmother's birthday, three days after her death. My mother never shed a tear for all the precious china broken that night; in fact, she told me that she was grateful. It had cleared the air.

How does one deal with such a veritable treasure ship stuffed with ghosts?

One can ignore and suppress them, beyond the occasional wry commentary, struggling throughout life against internal obstacles that paralyze and stifle action. One can absorb them, groom them like precious collector's items, and feed on them as one might feed on an addictive substance with a hunger that can never be satisfied. And one can totter along a middle route between the sirens of escapism and avoidance on the one hand and an obsessive unquenchable fascination on the other, trying to achieve a working relationship with this perilous internal inventory.

Ten years after my mother's death, my son reminded me of a German custom. It appeared in one of his "random fact of the day" posts on his Facebook page.

"They celebrate Halloween in Germany, but as a time to honor and respect the dead. One tradition is to hide all the knives in the house, for fear that returning spirits might injure themselves on any knives that are left out."

It seems like good advice.

Be nice to your ghosts, whether they are your own or your inherited ones. Your ghosts can't help themselves. Treat them like you would treat a rescue dog. Don't allow them on your bed. Teach them not to steal. Create a safe place for them. Take care of them gently. And don't overindulge them with attention, but instead, give them periods of rest and quiet. Then they won't take over your house.

EPILOGUE
WHAT REMAINS

OUR LIVES ARE FILLED WITH SACRED OBJECTS. I DON'T MEAN just the ones we consider perfect such as the first snowsuit I remember wearing when I was four; it was bright red and glorious, and it made me feel invincible. Sacred objects include things that are broken, bent, dented, worn to shreds— we love them for their imperfection.

In my basement, there are boxes filled with letters from several generations of family members. I even have an old leather briefcase bulging with our childhood scribbles. Sometimes I wish a kind spirit would come in the middle of the night and take the letters away. So far I have found discarding them impossible.

These letters are painful and treasured stand-ins for the people I loved. They occupy the same emotional space as some of the numerous inherited sacred objects in my possession, both the tangible ones and those that exist solely in my mind.

When I was a child, my mother gave me a book to read, *The Standard* by Alexander Lernet-Holenia. It describes the last days of the Austro-Hungarian Empire and a young officer's obsession with its military flags. They symbolize the world he had known as much as that world's death and decay. The silken fabric with its colors, faded and worn, haunt him even after he watches the flags being burnt in a courtyard in Vienna after the collapse of the empire. They whisper to him of all who died trying to protect them. Growing up in a family steeped in history, this story became part of my repertoire of nightmares—the vision of those faded silks whispering and wavering in the wind a sacred object of the imagination.

Over the years, this same image acquired a physical manifestation in the form of six silk ribbons from Christa's childhood. Miraculously, they survived the war, wrapped in thin tissue paper, and she clung to them until the end of her life. Every year at Easter, Christa decorated the breakfast table with an array of flowers, small wooden figurines bearing flutes, trumpets, and cymbals from the Harz Mountains, boiled eggs we had painted with watercolors, and most importantly, an array of frail silk ribbons in muted colors of grey, pale blue, green, purple, yellow, and red, laid across the center of the table like a web of multicolored veins.

Now, these ribbons reside in a drawer in my house, and I take them out at Easter, always afraid they will finally fall apart altogether.

There are other such objects—too many to name them all. Here I might mention my father's chapeau claque, a formal black silk hat from pre-World War II days. He wore it on the occasion of Winston Churchill's funeral in 1965, when he joined the German delegation sent to England in Churchill's honor. We loved to watch my father demonstrate how the hat would collapse into a flat shape and reopen with a resounding clacking noise, evoking an elusive but no less fascinating world of elegance and charm.

Then there was Christa's vintage kitchen scale, complete with a little family of brass weights, originally the property of her parents' cook Lajos in Warsaw.

One of the funniest of sacred objects was a plastic spoon

with a broken-off handle in Christa's flour jar. She insisted on keeping it out of a perverse frugality. Agostino and I searched for it after she had died, but it had vanished as had the "holy fork." This fork, a generously shaped implement with crooked tines, originally part of a set of so-called ship silver from my great-grandfather Tirpitz, was Christa's favorite fork in the kitchen. She used it for everything—stirring soup, whipping egg whites, and mixing herbs into her herb butter. I can see her standing in the kitchen in front of a bowl with heavy cream and rapidly flicking the fork back and forth.

"Watch me," my mother said when I tried it unsuccessfully. "You have to use your wrist."

Even years later, my brother was still upset that we couldn't find that fork.

Books also turned into sacred objects. My parents' house was filled with an enormous collection of books—so many that it was difficult to keep them all. On the other hand, getting rid of them was just as difficult. Certainly, disposing of books with one's grandfather's or great-grandfather's *ex libris* glued inside presents a challenge, and many come with inscriptions, often witty and amusing.

Funny, annoying, and endearing were the books in which my Hassell grandmother added her corrections by vigorously crossing out words she did not like or considered too risqué, underlining others she found thrilling, and liberally annotating everything she ever read. My father used to joke about her fondness for words like "brave," "knight," and "noble" while she disapproved of any words referring to sex. Even the word "pregnancy" was not allowed. "I could never figure out how she managed to produce four children," my father would say, his face crinkled with amusement. Confronted with her spikey lettering in old leather-bound volumes and the thick lines in black ink with which she crossed out text portions, I promised myself that I would never write into any book, not even the cheapest paperback.

To multiply the emotional weight of these books, my father had the habit of sticking notes in between the pages. He used recycled bits of scrap paper, the back of bills, and the like, to write commentary or to add his explanations on a particular detail. When I come across any one of these scraps, they immediately evoke my father's presence. I can visualize his amusement and his absorption in historical details as he was writing.

What does one do with all this?

"I wish someone would light a match under it," Christa sometimes exclaimed when frustrated by the sheer volume of family papers and books in my father's library. Yet, she did not do anything about the boxes of letters written to her during the war and later, leaving them for us to find.

The quintessential sacred object from Christa is the Golden Album. It is a collection of photographs, carefully preserved in a pale golden leather binder. The photographs consisted of images of people and places associated with the estate in Pomerania where Christa spent part of her child-hood. The Golden Album was among the items that my grandmother managed to bring to the West with her. All the years of my childhood I heard about it, and in my mind it acquired mythical proportions, turning into the equivalent of a key to the magical kingdom that was Muttrin—Christa's childhood home of which she told us so many unforgettable stories.

It resided in my grandmother's apartment. But she never let us look at it. Once when I was a teenager, returning to Germany for a few weeks, I screwed up my courage and asked whether I could see it. Reluctantly, she agreed to take it out of its drawer. I wanted to study it at my leisure but was afraid of my grandmother's restless presence next to me and her evident unwillingness to let me linger over it or to tell me more about particular photos.

It was a perplexing experience. I caught glimpses of pages

filled with faded photographs, many of which were familiar to me, followed by empty pages. Disappointed, I leafed through the album. The imagined key to the magical kingdom turned out to be rusty, bent, and brittle, and the glimpse of the land beyond the gate showed an empty landscape. I had been better off with Christa's stories and her intense, glowing eyes as she spoke about Muttrin.

Sacred objects are treasures and burdens at the same time. The phrase by Goethe about needing to earn for oneself the things one inherits to truly own them, so central to the lessons Christa learned in her childhood about the meaning of work, privilege, and ownership, is followed by another line just as meaningful.

"Those things that you don't use turn into a heavy burden."

Perhaps Goethe had not intended a literal application of his phrase; however, I came to appreciate it, especially because after Christa's death, we had to decide what to do with a vast amount of "stuff." Once again, as so often in my childhood, I found myself wishing that my mother had not managed to salvage anything and instead had been forced to begin from scratch. I loved some of the remnants of her life as much as I found myself overwhelmed by the physical embodiment of experiences and passions not of my own making. How does one dispose of or give away hundreds of items all of which bear some sort of emotional significance, weighted down by ghosts of the past?

Yet, Christa, for all her insistence that we should learn to appreciate and to value some of the items in her possession, also provided me with clues for dealing with this inheritance. Throughout her life, she insisted on using whatever she owned or had been able to rescue. When she could not do so, she passed them on to someone else.

"Keep what you will use and give away what other people

need or will use," Christa used to say. Firmly adhering to her pragmatic approach, it became manageable. Remembering her attitude about loss and about the need to move forward helped to free me as I went about the process of going through her possessions.

Meanwhile, one can also think of Goethe's phrase as all the inherited thoughts and memories that float around in one's conscience. If you do not have a proper place for them, they threaten to overtake you, leaving no room for anything else.

For us, sacred objects became a replacement language of sorts—a medium for expressing loss, grief, joy, confusion, fear, and love precisely because we were uncomfortable with talking about any such emotions.

What remains?

The work of emerging from Christa's orbit is an ongoing process. I still grapple with the question of how to deal with the combined weight of history and other people's lives like footprints in my soul. What does one do with the inherited detritus of existence in the form of a looming history populated by one's forebears, trunkloads of letters, and a veritable mountain of sacred objects seemingly impossible to dig out from under?

I found that buried inside that same mountain of an overwhelming past, there are keys to how to move beyond it. In 1951, WU gave Christa an edition of Dietrich Bonhoeffer's letters written from prison. In a letter to a friend on Christmas Eve in 1943, Bonhoeffer talks about loss:

"[G]ratitude transforms the agony of memory into silent joy. One does not carry the beauty from the past in one's heart like a thorn, but rather like a precious gift in itself. One must beware of wallowing in memories and surrendering oneself to them, just as one should not continuously contemplate a precious gift, instead only taking it out at special moments, while at other times keeping it safe like a hidden treasure that no one can take away. Then and only then the past will be a sustained source of joy and strength." (Bonhoeffer, 1951, p. 131).

Christa understood this and lived her life accordingly.

It helps to remember this when attempting to come to terms with the loss of a loved person. It also is a good roadmap for dealing with inherited memories, both good and bad ones.

Christa left me with a legacy of treasures of the mind and the imagination, a wealth of thoughts, interests, and passions. Most of all, she provided me with the equivalent of the keys to the kingdom of contentment and happiness. These keys were her capacity for finding joy by being open to small and large moments of pleasure, her insistence that a life well lived involved a form of performance art to help you over the rough spots, using the tools of discipline, grace, and a sense of humor, and an unquenchable willingness to work at everything that she undertook.

Christa liked to quote a line from the Luther Bible version of the 90th Psalm.

Unser Leben währet siebzig Jahre, und wenn's hoch kommt, so sind's achtzig Jahre, und wenn's köstlich gewesen ist, so ist es Mühe und Arbeit gewesen; denn es fährt schnell dahin, als flögen wir davon.

Having lived in America for most of my life, I have come to appreciate the King James Bible and the way the words roll thunderously across one's tongue. However, when looking up the English version of the 90th Psalm, I was disappointed.

The days of our years are threescore years and ten; and if by reason of strength they be fourscore years, yet is their strength labour and sorrow; for it is soon cut off, and we fly away.

Compelling as those uncompromising lines are, they don't include a word for describing life as *köstlich*, translated as exquisite or delicious so that you can almost taste the sweetness on your lips. For Christa, the 90th Psalm referred to a life that is indeed *köstlich* if one is willing to accept the toil and the labor.

Our life lasts seventy years, and at the very most eighty years, and if it has been delicious, it has been toil and labor; for it passes like the wind as if we were flying way.

Christa loved that line, and she lived it every day of her life. She put an effort into every single one of her actions. She was happiest when she was working and meeting the challenges she encountered. And she loved her life, embracing all the sorrow and labor of it with open eyes while never forgetting to be grateful for what was given to her.

I am left with the memory of Christa—dominant, exacting, controlling, stubborn, who never gave up and never gave in—utterly exasperating and exhilarating, and whom I loved.

I know that missing her is the last gift of her life, and I am thankful. She taught me that.

And yet there are times I would give anything to watch my mother's eyes glow once again with pleasure while telling a story about her exploits. I would give anything to have my mother walk into my house one more time, with her eagle eye noting any changes and with the tip of her finger adjusting a picture frame on the wall, while my son runs around the corner calling her name, "Mima, Mima," and insists that she play monopoly with him. I would give anything to once again be that little girl with a tendency to get hopelessly lost in the small town of Bonn, waiting at the street corner for my mother to come and pick me up, eagerly anticipating that moment when she would see me and embrace me with her smile, and I would be glad because the world had righted itself again.

PHOTOS

Postcard showing Muttrin linden tree, circa 1920. The inscription reads: "Greetings from Muttrin"

Christa, on the left, with Hans-Melchior, front right, and cousins in Muttrin, Pony Peter pulling the carriage, about 1932

Muttrin, circa 1920

Christa's maternal grandfather, Friedrich-Karl von Zitzewitz

Christa's maternal grandmother, Emmy von Zitzewitz

Erika von Studnitz, circa 1930

Bogislav von Studnitz, circa 1936

Christa, second from left, with cousins in Muttrin, circa 1936

Christa with grandmother Emmy von Zitzewitz in Muttrin, circa 1937

Christa, circa 1939

Hans-Melchior von Studnitz, circa 1941

Christa, 1942

Heinrich Hartmann, 1943

Christa in Tübingen, 1943

Egloff von Tippelskirch, 1944

Wedding of Christa and Egloff, December 28, 1944

Christa, about 1950

Wolf Ulrich von Hassell, about 1951

PHOTOS

Wedding of WU and Christa, March 29, 1952

Christa with Agostino, 1953

Christa in Rome, with WU on the left laughing at her, circa 1956

From left, Adrian, Agostino, and Malve 1960

WU, circa 1966

Christa in Ischia, Italy, 1966

Christa in Southampton, 1988

Christa in Florence, 1996

WU, October 1998

Malve with her son Ivan, 2001

Christa, 2003

Adrian, 2005

Agostino, 2007

Christa with Ivan in Southampton, 2008

Christa with daughter-in-law Elizabeth in Southampton, August 7, 2009, after the church service for Adrian, one week before her death

SOURCES

Note to reader Unless otherwise noted, all excerpts of texts and poems in German cited in this work have been translated by the author.

Arnim, Achim von (1781 – 1831), "Gebet" in Ludwig Reiners, ed., Der ewige Brunnen: Ein Hausbuch deutscher Dichtung. C.H. Beck Verlag, Munich, 1959.

Arnim, Elizabeth von, Elizabeth and Her Garden. Amazon.com Services LLC. May 12, 2012. P. 90.

Baumann, Hans, "Es zittern die morschen Knochen" German folksong, written in 1932 and adopted as the official marching song of the Reichsarbeitsdienst in 1935.

Benjamin, Walter, "Ninth Thesis on the Philosophy of History" in Illuminations: Essays and Reflections. Translation by Harry Zohn, New York: Schocken Books, 1969: 249.

Bonhoeffer, Dietrich, Widerstand und Ergebung. Briefe und Aufzeich-nungen aus der Haft. Herausgegeben von Eberhard Bethge, Chr. Kaiser Verlag, Munich, 1951.

Claudius, Matthias und Daniel Chodowiecki, Sämtliche Werke: Nach dem Text der Erstausgaben 1775 - 1812 und den Originaldrucken. Artemis & Winkler, Düsseldorf, 1996.

Cohen, Leonard, "Who by fire." Leonard Cohen's version of the Hebrew prayer "Unetanneh Tokef", chanted on Yom Kippur.

Gerhardt, Paul, "Geh aus mein Herz und suche Freud," text for a popular hymn, 1653, in Evangelisches Gesangbuch für Rheinland und Westfalen, Verlag W. Crüwell, Dortmund, 1901. Translation by Catherine Winkworth, 1855, in Lyra Germanica, Wentworth Press, 2016.

Goethe, Johann Wolfgang von, Faust I. Anaconda Verlag, Cologne, 2012.

Goethe, Johann Wolfgang von, "Der Erlkönig" in Goethes Werke in Zwölf Bänden, erster Band, Gedichte I. Aufbau-Verlag Berlin und Weimar, 1966.

Goncharov, Ivan, Oblomov. Penguin Classics; Revised edition, 2005).

Hassell, von, Fey, Hostage of the Third Reich. Scribner, 1989.

Hassell, von, Ulrich, Vom anderen Deutschland. Aus den nachgelassenen Tagebüchern 1938- 1944. Atlantis Verlag, Zurich, 1946.

Hassell, von, Ulrich, Der Kreis schließt sich - Aufzeichnungen aus der Haft 1944, ed. by Malve von Hassell (Ulrich von Hassell's memoirs written in prison in 1944) Propyläen Verlag, Berlin, 1994.

Jammes, Francis, The Romance of the Rabbit, translated from the French by Gladys Edgerton. Nicholas L. Brown, New York, 1920. P. 62.

Le Carré, John. Tinker, Tailor, Soldier, Spy, UK, Coronet Books, London, 1989.

Lernet-Holenia, Alexander, Die Standarte. Fischer Taschenbuch, Frankfurt, 2016.

Lessing, Gotthold Ephraim, Minna von Barnhelm oder das Soldatenglück: Ein Lustspiel in 5 Aufzügen. De Gruyter, Berlin, 1900.

Martin Luther Bibel, 1545, Psalm 90:10.

King James Bible, 1611, Psalm 90:10.

Klemperer, Victor. LTI. Notizbuch eines Philologen. Reclam, Leipzig, 1978.

Meyer, Conrad Ferdinand. Gustav Adolfs Page. Philipp Reclam Jun Verlag GmbH, Leipzig, 1900.

Münchausen, Börries Freiherr von, "Der goldene Ball" in Das Balladenbuch des Freiherrn Börries von Münchhausen. Deutsche Verlags-Anstalt, Munich, 1924.

Plicka, Karel, Prag: ein Fotografisches Bilderbuch. Artia; First Edition, 1953.

Rilke, Rainer Maria, "Herbstag" and "Das Karusell" in Gedichte. Insel Verlag, Frankfurt, 2006.

Schiller, Johann Christoph Friedrich von. "Reiterlied" from Wallenstein - Die Trilogie. Jazzybee Verlag, Altenmünster, 2015.

Shakespeare, William (1564-1616), Sonnets.

Strassmann, Ingolf, Die Geschichte der Familien Cohn, Bucky und Levy. E. Reinhold Verlag Altenburg.

Alfred Lord Tennyson, The Poetical Works Of Alfred, Lord Tennyson. Palala Press, 2015.

Unetanneh tokef, prayer for atonement on Yom Kippur, The Koren Yom Kippur Mahzor: [Hebrew/English High Holiday prayerbook.] Sacks, Jonathan, 1948- (Rohr family ed.). Jerusalem: Koren Publishers. 2012.

Wellershoff, Maria, Von Ort zu Ort: Eine Jugend in Pommern. DuMont Buchverlag GmbH & Co. KG, Cologne, 2010.

ACKNOWLEDGMENTS

Undoubtedly my mother would have favored me with one of her stern looks if she could have seen this book. Yet, I hope that she would know that it was a labor of love and a wholehearted attempt to honor her life.

Several friends and editors read the manuscript at various stages of its inception, in particular, Christine von Arnim, Dagmar von Winterfeld, William Greenleaf, Don Weise, Carrie Cantor, and Betty Lou Harmison. I am grateful for their kindness and their invaluable constructive criticism. May they forgive me for choosing to ignore some of their comments.

In addition to a wealth of papers and letters in the basement of my house, I drew on a range of resources at libraries and research institutes. I am particularly grateful to the Landesarchiv Thüringen as well as the Staatsarchiv Altenburg for their generous help in verifying details; this help was especially welcome since the pandemic made it difficult for me to travel to Germany to review some original sources myself. I owe enormous thanks to Miika Hannila and the Next Chapter Publishing team for bringing this project to life.

Meanwhile, ultimately there are two people whom I want to thank above all others, Wolf Ulrich von Hassell and Christa von Hassell, whose stories and wisdom and laughter have enriched me beyond measure and whose love continues to sustain me throughout all the days of my life.

Dear reader,

We hope you enjoyed reading *Tapestry Of My Mother's Life*.
Please take a moment to leave a review, even if it's a short one.
Your opinion is important to us.

Discover more books by Malve von Hassell at https://www.
nextchapter.pub/authors/malve-von-hassell

Want to know when one of our books is free or discounted?
Join the newsletter at http://eepurl.com/bqqB3H

Best regards,
Malve von Hassell and the Next Chapter Team

ABOUT THE AUTHOR

Malve von Hassell was born in Italy and spent part of her childhood in Belgium and Germany before moving to the United States. She is a freelance writer, researcher, and translator. She holds a Ph.D. in anthropology from the New School for Social Research and has taught at Queens College, Baruch College, Pace University, and Suffolk County Community College. Working as an independent scholar, she published *The Struggle for Eden: Community Gardens in New York City* (Bergin & Garvey 2002) and *Homesteading in New York City 1978-1993: The Divided Heart of Loisaida* (Bergin & Garvey 1996). She has edited her grandfather Ulrich von Hassell's memoirs written in prison in 1944, *Der Kreis schließt sich - Aufzeichnungen aus der Haft 1944* (Propylaen Verlag 1994). She published two children's picture books, *Letters from the Tooth Fairy* (Amazon KDP, 2012/2020), and *Turtle Crossing* (Amazon KDP, 2021), and her translation and annotation of a German children's classic by Tamara Ramsay, *Rennefarre: Dott's Wonderful Travels and Adventures* (Two Harbors Press, 2012). *The Falconer's Apprentice* (namelos, 2015) was her first historical fiction novel for young adults. She also published *Alina: A Song for the Telling* (BHC Press, 2020), set in Jerusalem in the time of the Crusades, and *The Amber Crane* (Odyssey Books, 2021), set in Germany in 1645 and 1945. She is working on a historical fiction trilogy featuring Adela of Normandy. You can read more about her work at

https://www.malvevonhassell.com.

Printed in Great Britain
by Amazon